BING AND OTHER THINGS

Bing

and Other Things

by Kathryn Crosby

Meredith Press   New York

Contents

Illustrations

BING AND OTHER THINGS

CHAPTER 1

Before Bing

"All right, girls, get ready."

How excited I was. I was born excited, and this day I was going to prove that I could be Miss Texas.

It was a beautiful warm day in Galveston, and from the pool I could see the Gulf shimmering in the distance. I pulled the royal-blue bathing suit up at the top, down at the thighs, and marched on stage behind that big girl from Midland. The music was gay, the judges sympathetic. Why, Bob O'Donnell was there, and he was head of Interstate Theatres, a man from the movies. And Mr. Nick Hilton, and glamorous Mrs. Sam Maceo, whose husband owned the Pleasure Pier, where the beauty contest was taking place, were judges too. And the contest was a big one—Miss Texas!

"Miss Kathryn Grandstaff, West Columbia." There was a smattering of applause, more than I'd hoped for. I looked far back in the auditorium and thought I saw my handsome big brother, Emery, leading the group. My chin went up a little, my smile spread from ear to ear. All the Grandstaffs were there, and they were for me, and the Stokelys from Lake Jackson too, and Aunt Frances Sullivan from Robstown. I'd *have* to win.

We had driven the sixty miles from West Columbia to Galveston the day before. West Columbia had been the first capital of the Republic of Texas. It had a population of 3,500, white frame houses along a main street with only a few stores, the Baptist and

Methodist churches, the schoolhouse where Mom taught, and the good farm-to-market roads that Daddy had built during his terms as County Road Commissioner.

My sister, Frances Ruth, had helped me pack for this trip. She had showed me the exaggerated Russian wolfhound stance she had learned when she took her Barbizon modeling course in New York. I didn't dare use her silver eyeshadow, though. Somehow that made me look ghostly instead of mysterious. She was four years older than I—twenty-two—and sophisticated enough to handle exotic things like that.

I minced offstage and exited to the wings. Frances was right there. "Kathryn, you were wonderful, but for heaven's sake try to keep your chest out farther than your stomach. The debutante slouch is all finished."

"I'm trying, Frances, I'm trying. Oh, but why am I so little! Why can't I be five foot seven like you? It's so much better for a model."

The other young ladies were making their entrances, so tall and lovely—and such nice girls. We would be three days in the contest, then the winner (I smiled smugly) would be crowned.

Frances and I sat in a corner of the dressing room. "Nervous?" she whispered.

"Not really." No, not really, if familiarity could alleviate fear.

I had been in my first beauty contest at age three. Aunt Frances and Uncle Leon Sullivan had entered me then as "Splash Day Princess" in Corpus Christi's Buccaneer celebration. Auntie nearly collapsed on the day of the contest because the committee, to enable spectators to see the toddlers, had built a runway for us seven feet from the ground. I can still hear Auntie yelling, "Kathryn, be careful. Don't fall off; don't fall off!"

I didn't fall. I loved it—loved the high ramp, the music, the excitement, and I absolutely adored scaring Aunt Frances. I teetered toward the edge, grinning with fiendish delight, caught the attention of the judges, and won the day. Auntie was so relieved she didn't even spank me.

Auntie and Uncle had taken me down to Corpus Christi to stay with them in a warmer climate where I could recover from a spring bout with pneumonia.

When Auntie and Uncle took me back up the coast to West Columbia, Mamma was shocked. She'd never dreamed her baby daughter was a bathing beauty. She knew her son Emery at age ten was a fine boy, blond and gentle, who sometimes forgot to milk our cow, old Pet, before he walked down the dirt road to school. She knew Frances Ruth, seven, was about the sweetest girl alive with a delicate slender frame that went to elbows and knees, and golden ringlets that when first trimmed had straightened for ever after. Frances was the family beauty, no doubt about that. I was "Daddy's Dumpling," a sweet euphemism for fat; nobody needed to worry about my elbows and knees. I didn't have any.

But I was active and infused with irrepressible zeal. My big stunt was to climb the ladder to check Henny Penny's nest for eggs in the tree by the back door. Often I'd fall somewhere on the way back, and the eggs would suffer. I'd take my cup out to the barn while Emery was milking to coax him for warm milk.

Emery was my hero, but he was going to grow up and marry Frances Ruth, so he had no time for the likes of me. Just to tantalize me, he'd aim one stream of warm milk in my cup, the next one in my face.

Auntie and Uncle brought me back home, "Splash Day Princess" at three. It had been an exciting year, a big year all around. Daddy and some friends had been building our house since January; it was to be ready for occupancy on April 1. It was right near the school, with big trees for me to climb and a wilderness adjoining us so old Pet could graze on open range and the flock of semitame mallards could wander out there, far from "civilization."

Auntie and Uncle, who were with us every Christmas and every Easter, and who had us stay with them many summers, joined the general jubilation over moving-in day. By West Columbia standards the Grandstaff manse was imposing with its two stories, Cape Cod gables, and a stairway leading up to the bedrooms. I wasn't used to stairs and proved it three times before the first day was out —plopping like a big batch of Mamma's biscuit dough from top to bottom.

Later on Mom and Dad were to add a back porch, then a wash room at the side of the kitchen, then another garage. Their bedroom was big and beautiful with its double bed. Emery had his own room, and Frances and I shared a room.

This was our home, and I thought it palatial. Oh, it was not an antebellum home like the Hogg Mansion nor a colonial plantation like the Underwood or T. M. Smith places on the Brazos, nor as important as Miss Kitty Nash Groce's ranch just out of town; but whatever Easterners thought, not every Texan was oil-rich. Though, as a matter of fact, Grandpa owned a few shares of Texas Company stock. He worked for the company, first as foreman of a roustabout crew, later as assistant to the Superintendent of Production.

You might say both the Grandstaffs and the Stokelys were "in oil," though Grandpa Stokely, after coming from Oklahoma as a thirteen-year-old, had worked on the railroad (Houston East and West Texas Line) as a member of the bridge gang, making ties, for the colossal sum of five dollars a day.

His brother, Edgar Stokely, had been a Deputy U.S. Marshal in the Oklahoma Territory, in those days a parlous occupation. He lived only to the ripe old age of twenty-seven. It seems that he tried to keep a posse from shooting an outlaw in front of the outlaw's mother and sister. He didn't want to upset their sensitivities. The outlaw had no sensitivity at all and promptly gunned down Grandpa's brother.

The family had been "in oil" from the time Mother was a little girl. Mother was the eldest daughter, and when they lived at Moonshine Hill, she had attended a one-room schoolhouse. Later, when they lived in Humble, she cooked breakfast at four thirty in the morning so Grandpa could get to work in Mr. Hine's Overland, one of the few cars in Humble. Then Mother and Aunt Frances cleaned the house and fixed lunches before they went off to school. At the time Grandmother wasn't feeling well after childbirth.

Daddy was born in Pollock, Louisiana, near Alexandria. He had two sisters, Ruth and Georgia. He and his brother, Uncle Buck, used to catch wild hogs on Caddo Lake. When they caught them, they'd crop them—split their ears, and give them an underbit—a sort of brand.

Daddy met Olive Stokely in Humble High School when he was a senior and she a sophomore. He knew at once that she was the girl for him. Then, six weeks before graduation, we entered World War One, and Dad went to Houston immediately and became a Marine—in "A" Company, a MacLemore Marine, "the Best of the Best," they called themselves.

All his friends were counseled to care for his girl, but not to forget that she was going to marry him one day. After two years Dad came back and found Mother with plenty of friends but totally undated—just as he had planned.

On September 30, 1920, the marriage license was purchased with the Gold Quarter-Eagle that Dad had won in a high school 880-yard dash. As he tells the story, Dad had invited Mom to a circus, but all the tickets were gone, so what else could they do but get married? There wasn't much time. Grandpa Stokely was being transferred by the Texas Company to the new field in West Columbia, and of course the others were moving with them.

They went to a going-away party for Mother's family, and after that woke up a clergyman friend, and, with two classmates as witnesses, they were married. Daddy then walked Mother home, said good-night, and disappeared until she could break the news gently to Grandma.

Grandma and Grandpa Stokely weren't surprised. They'd received a beautiful letter that Daddy had written asking for Mamma's hand, and besides that he had promised he was going to amount to something. Why, he had been a rig builder when he was only seventeen. He'd worked with his father in Louisiana, and in the Humble area of Texas, for Dann Gunn, a famous oil-field name of that time.

Dad's father, Lewis Grandstaff, had come from Ohio as a young man. His most illustrious relative was an Indian scout named Louis Wetzel, a first cousin, who was called Death Wind by the Indians. It was said his guns were never unloaded.

Soon after Dad and Mom were married they moved to West Columbia. Rig builders made good wages, but the risk was high.

Dad sized up the situation pretty accurately one day when he said, "Ollie, there are some pretty fine men out in the field; they work hard, but most of them don't have much to fall back on if there's an accident or the well plays out. Why, Elmer Hobbs is nearly sixty—he's worked all over the country drifting from one field to another and he doesn't have a nickel to his name. I'd like to go to college, and I think you'd like college too. That way we'd both have a future."

They went to the town banker and outlined their plan. They'd go to school in the summer and teach in the winter. It took them a good ten years. Dad got his Bachelor's degree in 1929, but Mother, because of having children and other feminine preoccupations, could only get a permanent teaching certificate, but she was persistent, like all my family, and finally earned her B.A. in 1950 and her Master's in 1961.

So they were pleased to have a Splash Day Princess of three in the family, but a little worried that I had begun a career before I had even gone to school. It happened in May, and during the next school year, Katharine Douglas, the third-grade teacher, created an original play called "The Toy Maker's Dream," and who should play the Dream and sing "On the Good Ship *Lollipop*" but me.

Soon my theatrical career faded into the normal, but to me it was wonderful growing up in a little town in Texas. I ran off about every other day to visit Nancy Jim Slaughter, who had a huge stack of funny books not allowed in our house, and whose mamma always had a big jar of candy bars, which she dispensed with generosity.

At the other end of the block lived redheaded Dolores Gupton, my dearest friend. Her grandmother, who was called "Mamma Stucker," was a teacher and watched over all of us neighborhood kids, making sure that we wore our sweaters even in the summertime, breaking up smell-melon battles that took place in the woods behind the house (girls against the boys—and we nearly always won), trying to get us out of trees where we got stuck, and telling us to behave like ladies. A fruitless admonition, I fear.

Dolores' uncle was a Texas rancher—not on a scale with the Kings or Klebergs, but pretty big stuff for West Columbia. They had lots of cattle and horses, and one old swaybacked nag that Dolores and I would ride bareback on hot summer days. We also climbed the oak trees out at their place, big ones with limbs that grew into the ground and then skyward again.

When I was five, Miss Fay Carr came to live with us. She was a music teacher from Bay City, Texas, and she had come to West Columbia to teach piano. There was no hotel or place fit for a lady to stay, so Mother offered her the use of our home, and in return all of us—Emery, Frances, and I—were given piano lessons. Miss Carr had the most beautiful hands, very soft and gentle, white hair, and a happy smile, which persisted even through the yearly music exams in Houston.

After working with Miss Carr, first grade held no terrors at all, particularly with Miss Avera as my teacher. She was a wonderful woman, who taught me to love learning. I had such fun with her that they skipped me to the third grade, and then in fourth grade I fell under the magic spell of Miss Minnie Black, a Southern lady, very tall with washboard waves in her hair, and a soft drawl. She looked terribly old (she was probably sixty), and she made Texas history live. We were impressed with the magnitude of the fact that Stephen F. Austin caught pneumonia in West Columbia, and that the Josiah Bell plantation was just out of town. Miss Minnie had come up the Brazos in a steamboat that had put in at Belle's Landing in 1884. Her family got out into the mud and settled there. Later they built a big white mansion with real stained-glass windows down in East Columbia.

She never did explain the serious mistake made by those settlers. The Brazos was not a friendly river, it overflowed its banks every year, taking mud off one side and depositing it on the other. All those big white colonial houses with balconies on the second story and attics, and sometimes even a watchtower—they were all built on the wrong side of the Brazos. Year after year their backyards were eaten away until there was nothing left. Some houses, too, fell in the river. Finally there were just a few left, and East Columbia became practically a ghost town with only about three hundred people in it. West Columbia by comparison became a booming metropolis only two miles away.

We went to church every Sunday, winter and summer. I learned nearly all the verses of the New Testament, trying to save up points to get to go to the Baptist camp at Palacios, fifty miles from home. A lot of my theological study took place in the big hammock, strung between the pecan and the elm tree in the backyard. I used to lie there for hours, looking up through the leaves and dreaming. I was going to grow up one day and be a movie star—or a Chinese missionary. Not a missionary to China because that would have been too usual. I really thought that if I reached the Orient my eyes would become the lovely almond shape instead of the pop-eyed round that I was given by my Scotch, Irish, English, German and French heritage. I would then speak in the foreign tongue and convert everyone to the First Baptist Church of West Columbia.

When I got older, at least nine or ten, Mother and Dad would let me take the train from Brazoria, fourteen miles away, all the way down to Robstown by myself. They'd buy my ticket and give it to the conductor, and give me fifty cents, which I was hard put to spend between one station and the other. Usually I just stood in the vestibule of the car watching the trees whiz by.

Aunt Frances and Uncle Leon had settled in Robstown, seventeen miles from Corpus Christi, and Uncle Leon had the Bemis Bag Agency. He sold onion sacking and baskets for produce. Auntie and Uncle were always like a fairy godmother and godfather. They did such glorious things. They took Frances Ruth and Emery on a trip one summer to the White Sands, and the tales they told when they returned made me long to go too—camping out, riding horseback, seeing mountains. I'd never seen a mountain. Oh, in picture books, sure, but it didn't look the same. In West Columbia I stood in the middle of the prairie and turned around and knew the world was round—the horizon looked like a bowl upside down—with maybe an oak tree jutting up here and there. The horizon looked so easy to reach, so inviting. I wanted to go to the edge and keep going. I wanted to see what was on the other side of those oaks and pecan trees.

When I was nine, Auntie and Uncle said, "All right, it's your turn." My turn—and Mother said Yes, she could get away from home too. We were going to drive to Mexico City.

Right out of Laredo, I saw my first mountain—a big form looming up in the sky. Purple, sharp, jagged, beautiful, it was just like in the books. I thought it was a mountain, but it was only a foothill. Around Monterey came the first real peaks that could really be called *montañas,* but by then I was inured to the magic. There was so much to see, so much to know. The strange foods at the border —*cabrito* (barbecued goat), quail, papaya for dessert, and the strange language, the soft, lovely language which I had heard occasionally in Robstown. Then I realized: This was a foreign country.

In Mexico City we saw the pyramids, the "floating gardens." A guide took us everywhere, and he spoke Spanish and English. Why couldn't I speak English and Spanish? All I could speak was Texan. But before we left Mexico, I learned how to sing *"Ya se van los pastores."* The telephone operator at the hotel taught me how, and let me braid the trunk lines into the switchboard—with predictable results. She was trying to teach me how to do a French braid for my long brown pigtails.

I had always suspected it, but by the end of the Mexican trip, I knew that Uncle Leon was the most romantic, most handsome, most wonderful man that ever lived.

Our trip ended in Robstown. While Mother and Auntie repacked the clothes so that Mamma and I could take the afternoon train back to Brazoria and West Columbia, I went to the shed with Uncle Leon. He had to check up on the mail, and I went exploring in the rows and rows of baskets that were so much fun to climb, and jumped on the onion sacking, which made a lovely soft pillow. High up on one side of the shed there was loft, and in it were some old trunks where Auntie kept clothes, wonderful for dressing up— beaded gowns and beaded bags, and a feather boa or two.

I was exploring a little farther than I had ever before, when I found a small trunk that wasn't locked. I looked inside and there were the most exquisite baby clothes—all handmade, a beautiful little patchwork quilt, knitted bootees, a christening gown—long and white with a matching cap. Somehow I knew I had stumbled on something not meant for my eyes. I very carefully replaced the tissue paper and closed the trunk, and then I went into the office with Uncle.

I tried to be tactful about the whole thing and failed. I went to Uncle Leon and said, "What are those baby clothes doing up in the loft?"

Uncle looked at me for a minute, then leaned back in his chair, and said, "Well, Kathryn, I think you're old enough to know such things. Your Auntie and I wanted children very badly, and it seemed we couldn't have them, so a doctor in Corpus Christi helped make arrangements for us to adopt a baby through the adoption agency. We went over the day the baby was born, and saw him—he was beautiful, but terribly tiny. The doctor said he had a heart condition and would need very special care. Well, we didn't have the money to bring in special nurses, and your Auntie realized she couldn't do it all, though she was game to try. So we put those dreams away."

"Uncle Leon," I finally stammered out, "can I be your child— partly, I mean. I know I'm Mommy's and Daddy's and I love them very much; but they have Frances Ruth and Emery, too, and I love you so much, and . . . well, could I sort of be yours too?"

Uncle laughed. His blue Irish eyes crinkled with happiness, his ruddy cheeks flushing a little. He took me on his knee and said, "Well, Kathryn, your Aunt Frances and I have always felt you're partly our child. Now you do me a favor, hotshot; don't discuss this with Aunt Frances. We don't want to make her feel sad, do we?"

"Oh no, Uncle Leon, I wouldn't want to make her feel sad."

When Mom and I got home on the train the next day, there was big news: The schoolhouse had burned down. Some classes were being held in the gymnasium with little partitions between each noisy group of students. I was first going to class in the Methodist Church, and then, when some of the debris had been cleared away, in the cafeteria. Mother called Auntie to tell her of the horrible event, and Aunt Frances responded with characteristic directness, "Send Frances Ruth down here. She can't possibly learn anything in the gymnasium with all that noise."

"But Frances, you and Leon don't have room."

"We have two bedrooms, and that's plenty."

Frances Ruth was packed and by morning was on the train for Robstown. I don't know that Daddy liked it too much, having his pretty blond girl go away to school, but we all knew it was best for her. And I was so pleased because I got spoiled by Daddy that whole year. I got to go fishing; I got to cook with Mother; I took dancing, though we really couldn't afford the lessons; and I passed the fifth and sixth grades in one year.

And Emery came home from A&M, where he was studying. He was suddenly so grown up, and he treated me like a lady. I wanted to win his heart, but by now I knew that he couldn't ever marry his own sister, even if he'd given her that gorgeous Shirley Temple doll that he'd paid for at fifty cents a week, and which took him six months to earn.

Now, when the family gathered at Christmas time, it was a real family reunion. There were Auntie and Uncle and my sister, who was much nicer now that I didn't have to share my room with her every day. She was a tennis champion and dating the most handsome boy, and she loved Robstown High School. It was much bigger than West Columbia High School. Why, it was just as exciting as going away to Europe or something.

When I became a freshman, I simply announced to Aunt Frances and Uncle Leon, "It's my turn." Uncle grinned, but Mother and Daddy looked a little distressed. Then they started going into the intricacies, "Well, she could take dancing in Corpus Christi. Houston is sixty miles away, and it's much too far to go. And Olive, you're teaching school all day, so I can make her clothes for her, and Frances Ruth is back so you can give her all the spoiling you've been giving Kathryn—now that Emery is away in service."

I sat there grinning like a Cheshire cat—a real adventure was coming: I was going away to school. Everybody in West Columbia knew I was too young to be in the ninth grade, I was only twelve, and they were having dates and kissing and things like that, and I didn't really care about boys except maybe to play baseball with or climb trees with, or something.

It was to be a one-year arrangement. And the routine was quickly established. First thing in the morning once a week Auntie and I would be up at seven, drive to Corpus Christi, seventeen miles away, and I'd have a ballet lesson and change clothes in the back of the car on my way to make the ten o'clock algebra class. Home for lunch, English, General Science, Spanish, Civics—and, except for piano-lesson days, tennis. Because Frances Ruth had been a tennis champion, I thought I'd try, so the after-school hours were full of forehands, backhands, serves—hours of tennis, wearing out the tennis shoes until there was a hole where I dragged my right toe over the concrete when I served.

I made friends who would be dear to me all my life. There was Lee Parr, who was in my class and had the misfortune of being a raving beauty and a genius—an almost impossible combination, but she managed it. And Frances Smith, who lived down the block, with whom I made innumerable pots of Spanish rice. About the end of the freshman year I discovered that boys were really very nice after all, and I lost all inclination to climb trees, trying vainly to put up my hair smoothly. The pigtails had been cut a year ago, thanks to Uncle's suggestion, but I still couldn't cope with it at all.

At Christmas, James Bell Williams took me to my first formal. Auntie made me a gorgeous velvet bodice and plaid taffeta skirt, and I danced without stepping on it too much. Jim's parents drove us to the dance, then home again. And my mind was a fog with Auntie's admonition, "Wait until he opens the door for you," and Uncle's compliment, "Well you're not Daddy's Dumplin' any more: You're quite a young lady at thirteen."

After the dance, I told them all about it. "You couldn't believe how beautiful it was. The Teen Club was decorated with huge paper flowers and most of the freshmen girls came together. I was one of the few that had a date. And Taylor Nichols—a senior!— danced with me and asked about Frances Ruth, and a junior, Dougie Dunlap—he's *so* cute!—tried to teach me to jitterbug. I'm so glad I skipped those grades, because most of the girls are taller than the boys."

Soon that year was over, and then the next, and then I returned as a junior to be Assistant Editor of our annual under Frances Smith. At fifteen, lightning struck again. There was a Robstown

Country Club, and Aunt Frances and Uncle were members. To open the swimming pool, they had a beauty contest. All of us at school were entered, and Lee Parr's mother observed with great humor, "You girls all look like you're going down to the drugstore to get a Coke. Why don't you stand tall like those models and walk like you know what you're doing!"

Lee and I tried, and Aunt Frances was highly embarrassed when I won second.

The next week, Uncle Leon came home from Rotary Club and said, "We put names in a hat, and Kathryn's been drawn to represent the Rotary Club in the Buccaneer Navy Contest in Corpus Christi. How about that?"

I yelped with glee because five or six classmates had already been entered by the various organizations in town, and it would be such fun. We'd get to ride on a float and go to parties, and meet all the handsome midshipmen out at Cabaniss Naval Base.

A girl who had won several beauty contests and was a whole year older than I was told me to wave at the crowd when we were riding in the convertibles. But she didn't tell me what to do when I had an accident at tennis practice the day before we were to go to Corpus Christi. There was a sliced forehand that came at me hard, down the line, and I went for it, missed, and came up with two skinned knees.

Aunt Frances had made a pirate costume for me out of royal-blue satin with white blouse, with satin boot tops that would not stay put. The first time we marched across the platform, the boots started working their way off my feet, revealing my tennis-scarred knees. Right after me came a beautiful brunette with a parrot on her right shoulder, and a long scarlet cape.

There it goes, I thought. Anyone who can wear a cape and a parrot too has more poise than I can muster. Then it was time to watch the Blue Angels do their aerobatics. The midshipman who was driving three of us girls in the convertible watched me take off my disobedient blue boots, then grinned, saying "Barefoot girl with cheek. But you sure could talk when they asked you to up there."

"Oh, the problem isn't getting me to talk; it's getting me to shut up. Aunt Frances is always trying to do that."

A few minutes later an officer came over to the car and said rather gravely, "Miss Grandstaff, could you come to the platform, please."

Good heavens, I thought, was it illegal to have bare feet on an air base? I looked around frantically and didn't see another soul with bare toes. I yanked on the boots with what I hoped was dignity and limped up to the judges who were sitting there in a serious semicircle.

"I only took them off for a minute . . ." I started to say.

"You what? What do you mean? You've just been chosen as Miss Buccaneer Navy."

The Blue Angels zoomed over just then, and I could have hopped aboard their jets without their even slowing down.

I signed an autograph—three, really. My whole full name—Olive Kathryn Grandstaff. I was so excited. The girls were clustered around, all clutching each other as girls are wont to do at times like that. Aunt Frances came running up, and both of us were shrieking with delight. But out of the corner of my eye, I saw the boy on whom I had a huge crush look at me rather solemnly and walk the other way.

The ball at Cabaniss Base that night was a dream. All those handsome midshipmen in their uniforms, and a crown of sixteen orchids, a huge trophy (very hard to carry), and tickets for a trip for two to Mexico. I had caught the ring on the merry-go-round. It turned out to be brass.

A few days later at school, the boy who had looked so solemn, said, "I won't be calling you anymore, Kathryn. You seem to have changed since you won that thing over in Corpus Christi."

"How have I changed?"

"Maybe you haven't changed. Maybe I've changed." And he walked off. I went back to tennis with vicious determination. I even beat the number-one boy on the men's ladder—and then *he* wasn't my friend anymore.

I felt miserable. The dancing lessons went on, the piano lessons went on, but at school it was a kind of torture. There were several girls, nice girls from good families, and they had a club—and I wasn't in it. They used to do the most fascinating things, it seemed to me on the outside. They had luncheons during the school week, and they went shopping together, and rode around in cars and talked about—oh, probably about the most profound matters, about life and men—deep philosophical questions. I never knew. I wasn't included.

My plight seemed especially horrid since all the world was in love that year. My sister Frances, usually a sensible sort, had a date with an Air Force veteran from Rosenberg. They went to the beach at Freeport for a picnic and she returned starry-eyed.

"Kathryn, I'm in love. He threw an orange at me and it smashed all over my back!"

Ugh—that's love?

And Emery. He was in love with a beautiful blonde co-ed from San Marcos State Teachers College. He was so impressed with her lilting soprano voice, her sensitive nature and her love for him that he'd proposed and been accepted and married in December. I thought she was terribly nice, but very quiet and reserved. Frances and Leonard were wed in February. I was twice a bridesmaid— never a bride? Well, not for a long, long time.

Summer came, mercifully, and with summer came the prize trip to Mexico for Auntie and me. We flew all the way from Corpus Christi, going way out over the Gulf, crossing over Tampico, and landing in Mexico City.

We were met by a tour guide from the Aguirre Agency, who took us at once to the old Ritz Hotel, and there we had our beautiful room full of long-stemmed carnations, bunches and bunches of them. Mexico seemed exotic and gorgeous the first evening. Auntie and I were starved, so we thought we'd just step around the corner and get a bowl of chicken soup. The dining room seemed to be closed, it was nine thirty at night. As we walked along talking gaily, I noticed that there weren't any women on the street, though there were lots of men, looking at us and smiling. Isn't that friendly, I thought.

We stopped in a tiny café and had delicious *arroz con pollo,* a cross between a very thick soup and a very thin stew. The waiter and *patrón* looked a little nervous and there was much whispering in back of the counter; but all the other guests, who happened to be male, smiled at us.

Auntie had begun to look concerned, but I just smiled back. Perhaps they knew I was Miss Buccaneer Navy.

When we strolled back to the hotel, the kind man at the desk said, "If I may intrude, ladies, do not go out at night here—not without an escort. The appearance might not be just what you would desire, *señora* and *señorita.*" Aunt Frances turned an absolutely lovely crimson.

We withdrew in dignified silence after nodding our gratitude. Once in the room we locked the door, and roared. Imagine people thinking I might be—well, you know what. And Aunt Frances too! Well, nothing like that ever happened in Robstown or West Columbia. We were careful for the rest of the trip, but inclined to giggle.

Robstown High, during my senior year, was a triumph—for two excellent reasons. One was Catherine Kantz, our English teacher, and the other a young drama instructor named Martha Chambers.

Mrs. Kantz initiated me into a few of the mysteries and wonders of the English language—in play form, in novel form. She even made me like grammar. Miss Chambers not only worked on my voice, but cared enough to sit down with me and say, "Why do you stick your nose up in the air? Everybody's going to hate you if you're so snobbish."

"But Miss Chambers, I don't mean to be snobbish. I'm scared to death. You see, the girls don't like me. They never have, and I don't know what to say. If I speak, they won't answer me."

"Well, they certainly won't speak to you with that chip on your shoulder."

Had I wasted three whole years? I had been so sure they didn't like me. I never did give them a chance.

"Thank you, Miss Chambers. I do have a dear friend in Lee Parr."

"Yes, but she's the only one. Give the world a chance; it's not such a bad place. You might even grow to like it here."

The Chamber of Commerce called in December. Aunt Frances said, "Well, I'll ask her. Kathryn, do you want to try out for Rodeo

Queen of the Houston Fat Stock Show and Exposition? It'll be in Houston in February. But you have to ride a horse."

"Oh, Auntie, you know I can't ride a horse that well. Do you think Uncle would teach me?"

"Well, we can see."

Uncle was willing, and certainly able. Instead of tennis skinned knees I developed saddle sores. We rode daily. The rides were challenging because Bobby King's quarterhorse, Topsy, was the frisky type and seemed to know that I couldn't ride at all. He followed Uncle's lead, which was all right, I suppose, except that I never knew exactly what he was going to do. On those long, brisk, wintry afternoon rides, Uncle and I would talk about the future.

He was always the one I could talk with, dream with.

"Yes, Uncle, I do want to be a movie star, something over the mountains on the other side of the world. I'd love to see California —and China and Timbuctoo and Siam; but for a start California will do."

"Well, Kathryn, maybe after you finish school, you could go out west and take one of those stage dancing courses. They last six weeks or two months, and then, if you didn't make it in movies, you could always come back and teach dancing."

"Oh yes, Uncle, that would be the thing to do. And we wouldn't tell anybody about trying for the movies."

"Oh no, that wouldn't do. Sit up a little straighter. You look like the Hunchback of Notre Dame."

"But it hurts."

"That's because you're not sitting up straighter."

I tried. I'd do anything for Uncle, though both Topsy and I were well aware that I'd never be a horsewoman.

When we got to Houston, practically everyone seemed to have been born in the saddle. I've never seen so many accomplished horsewomen in my life. My brother-in-law's dad, Big Leonard, said, "Why, Kathryn, you haven't got a chance out there. There are girls there that can really ride."

I drew myself up to my full five feet two and said, "Topsy will give them a great show and I'll hang on."

Oh, that was a trip! We all went to Houston, and stayed at the Shamrock Hotel. Mr. Glenn McCarthy, who owned the hotel then, took all the contestants to lunch one day. I felt I was getting to know the kind of Texan the rest of the world feels Texas is full of—Glenn McCarthy made oil wells and hotels appear from nowhere.

Dr. Northway, the veterinarian of the legendary King Ranch in Kingsville, loaned us a beautiful tooled-leather saddle. We borrowed a riding habit from a friend, and bought a white twenty-gallon hat. This was it!

"And now representing the Robstown Chamber of Commerce —Miss Kathryn Grandstaff." The gates swung open and Topsy pranced out. He was not an easy horse to handle, and I was ashamed of his looks. Bobby King had bobbed his tail just the day before we came to Houston. I had thought it so gorgeous and silky, but Bobby assured me that all quarterhorses had their tails bobbed before they worked in the arena.

What Bobby didn't tell me was that Topsy was a tie-down pony used to chasing calves, and when that gate opened, he pranced out ready to go. It took him about two seconds to realize that there was nothing to chase, and it took me about two seconds to come down from my perch high in the air.

The huge arena was full of people—people from all over. There were ten of us girls, and I looked on with horror as a palomino stallion ran away. The girl had seemed to be a beautiful rider, yet she could hardly control her mount. A cowboy jumped off the fence, caught the reins, and stopped her.

A voice was saying, "Turn and canter." I was too busy waving at the Robstown cowboys to pay any attention to the judge's voice. Topsy heard him—he turned and cantered. Then the voice said, "Turn and walk." I don't know what happened to Topsy. He had never paid any attention to me, so why should he listen to a voice over a loudspeaker? But he turned and walked—mincingly, daintily, proudly, while I tried not to appear obvious as I clung to the saddle horn with my left hand and waved to friends with my right.

I felt like a little brown beetle in the middle of a pile of silver. There were so many white horses, so many silver trappings. But those palominos and those white stallions didn't really understand word signals like Topsy did. And none of them could prance so beautifully.

Now the horses were standing quiet—some of them, anyway. Topsy certainly was. The judges called a girl's name. She was the lovely blonde who rode like a whiz. She marched her horse forward, took off her hat and circled the arena. The applause was deafening. Out of the corner of my eye I noticed that when she put the hat back on, the applause stopped.

Then they called my name, and without waiting for a cluck from me, Topsy moved forward. I took off the big white hat and left it off—for several round trips. The cowboys laughed and the judges grinned, but the applause went on and Kathryn Grandstaff of Robstown became Rodeo Queen of the Houston Fat Stock Show—a title I shall never live down.

Uncle was waiting back in the corral when we trotted out of the arena. He caught me, and I hugged him, crying a bit. I was so excited and so happy. And just then a very dignified gentleman came up and said, "Hello, I'm Art Rush, Roy Rogers' agent. I wonder if you'd like lunch tomorrow? Do you have any ambitions to go to Hollywood?"

I was crying so hard, I could hardly see through the tears. Uncle had his arm around my shoulder, and said, "Of course."

Thank heaven Uncle was there. I could only blubber. He went on, "I think maybe lunch tomorrow would be a good idea. Kathryn seems a little excited now."

Practically every girl in Texas enters beauty contests. They never stop—festivals and pageants, and community projects and charity shows. It may be good citizenship to put on a bathing suit and get into the festivities, but you don't really have to risk your life aboard an adorable quarterhorse named Topsy. I hugged him. He was docile as a lamb now, and though he didn't drive away the Ford convertible—our prize—he knew who had won that contest.

Lunch the next day was like a dream—a happy dream. Mother and Dad and Auntie and Uncle were all there with us. Mr. Rush looked terribly distinguished and very important, and he wore his Masonic pin, which Daddy immediately noted.

"You know, Kathryn, at sixteen you're pretty young to try Hollywood," he said. "I think it might be wise to go to college for a couple of years—take some Drama courses, maybe get rid of your Texas accent."

"Do I have a Texas accent?"

"Kathryn, you and all the rest of the people who live in Texas have Texas accents."

"Well, what's wrong with that?"

"It's great if you want to play little girls from Texas."

"I see. Well, sir," and then the idea caught fire, "maybe I could go to the University of Texas and take a speech course and come right on out this summer."

"Well, as soon as you feel ready, just call and let me know."

We had a huddled family conference and agreed to keep it all a secret. We drove the little Ford convertible carefully down to Robstown and parked it in the garage. I didn't have a license, and I wouldn't have driven it to school even then. First, because I was a bad driver, and secondly, because I didn't want a repeat of the previous spring. If only I'd had a sense of humor, it all would have seemed funny—winning the contest but fearing what the other girls would say. I was so serious about life and my "career." And sure enough, right away they began to call me Miss Fat Stock.

It wasn't a repeat of the previous spring. It was worse! As Miss Buccaneer I'd been invited to the Robstown High Junior-Senior banquet by a senior and had a glorious time. We had danced until three in the morning, and Mother and Aunt Frances had been waiting up for my full report of the elegant chicken à la king in patty shells served at the Robert Driscoll Hotel. My faded corsage was pressed between the pages of a book to be saved for all eternity. Happy memories. But Miss Fat Stock received no calls from eager escorts to go to the banquet. Inexplicably I was a social pariah. Uppity? I never knew.

Thank heaven my father was in politics. An election came up the same week as this most important of the school's social events, and when the journalism teacher said, "Oh, come on, Kathryn, don't be stuffy. Come to the party anyway," I could say with a straight face, "I couldn't possibly come. I have to go home and help Daddy campaign. I've always done that, ever since I was five years old and he first made a race." Oh, I was so noble.

So noble, so self-sacrificing—that's how I looked. How I felt was all shriveled up inside, afraid to raise my head for fear somebody might look at me and smile, which would mean that they knew that I hadn't been invited to the party, and that I was running away because I was ashamed to stay in town and not go.

Auntie and Uncle put me on the train that weekend, and I took the long ride back up to Brazoria.

Politics quickly erased any other worries I might have had. The years had been full of challenges for Mom and Dad. He was now County Commissioner. He'd been elected for three two-year terms. This would be his fourth—we hoped.

Election day was hot. Mom and Frances Ruth and I put on comfortable clothes. Emery and his wife Netta went with Frances and Leonard in the loudspeaker truck. "Come out to the polls and vote. Vote for the man of your choice, but vote!"

Mom and Dad and I went down to the band hall and had a chance to get reacquainted with all the neighbors I hadn't seen for some years, while passing out little cards reading: *D. E. Grandstaff, Candidate for County Commissioner, Precinct No. 3. Your Vote and Support Appreciated.*

"Why, Kathryn, how are you?"

"Fine, Miss Probst. Haven't seen you since you taught me Sunday School. Hope you're going to vote for my Daddy. You know he's the man for the job."

"Kathryn, you know I wouldn't vote for anybody else—but don't let them hear me say that." She grinned and walked off to the polls with my card in her hand.

Meanwhile I was working away with my cards. "Hello, Dr. Berger. How have you been? Sure good to see you again. Say, you haven't seen me since I got my braces off. Those buck teeth don't stick so far out anymore, do they?"

The polls closed at six. It was good to feel some cool breeze on my sunbaked neck. My gabardine skirt and green blouse were all dusty, my feet ached, but I wasn't worried about the party anymore. Nothing could have been farther from my mind than the

Junior-Senior banquet. What really mattered was the outcome of this election.

Uncle Edgar and his wife Margaret had come over from Lake Jackson with a cold ham for supper. We ate standing up around the table—dead tired, afraid to talk. Then we went out to the football field and sat while they sprayed clouds of DDT to shoo the mosquitoes away. Mr. Mays wrote on the blackboard: *Damon— Old Ocean—West Columbia.* A few hand-counted votes from one precinct. Then from the next . . . And by ten o'clock the results were in. Dad had won! He thanked me and I was the happiest daughter in the world, except maybe for Frances Ruth, who might be happier only because she was bigger and older—well, and wiser, too.

It wasn't hard to go back to school that Monday morning. My dad had won the election, and I'd helped him. That was more important than a dance.

The rest of the spring flew by. High school graduation was solemn and dignified. Not so our Rainbow Girls Grand Inspection. Such a night! Our Mother Advisor, Beatrice Jackson, encouraged all of us and comforted us, but the girl who played Religion fainted, Hope tore her formal, and I, as Worthy Advisor, had to keep peeking at cue cards. If this school year ever ended and I lived, I felt I'd repair to my upstairs room in West Columbia and just sleep and sleep.

A while later my friends Frances Smith and Gina Nichols, who were home from the University of Texas, suggested I go back there with them for summer school. So I just took off my graduation gown and rushed to Austin.

I walked into Dr. Loren Winship's office in the Drama Department that hot summer of 1950 and said, "Dr. Winship, I want to take a course in theater so I can get rid of my Texas drawl— because . . . you see . . . I'm going to California to be a movie star."

Dr. Winship's eyes may have held a glint of amusement, but he didn't crack a smile. He said, "That's interesting—Miss . . . ah . . . . Grandstaff? Is that your name?"

"Yes."

"Miss Grandstaff, how long do you plan to stay with us?"

"Oh, just this summer. Just long enough to fix the accent."

"Well," he mused. "I think we have a drama course that might be good for you." He put me into Drama 405. It was the nastiest, dirtiest crew course in the entire curriculum. I swept floors, I sorted nails. And because they realized immediately that I wasn't safe with any of the power tools, I painted flats instead of building them. I also found assorted properties for the production of that summer session, *The Corn Is Green*.

It never occurred to me at the beginning that I had pulled a gaff, or used something less than a tactful approach, and by the end of six weeks, I was too tired to care. But I was hooked. Why, we'd done a show for Jack Kramer and all the professional tennis players! Word Baker and I had done a little dance. This was theater, and it was fun. Oh, it was fun!

When I got back home I immediately started to paint every piece of furniture in my room, using my new talents gleaned from Drama 405.

When the paint dried, Uncle Edgar offered to get me a job at Dow Chemical, because he felt my folks shouldn't have to foot all the bills all the time. But I had just heard that a famous ballet master was teaching in Houston. For the sum of $50 I could take ten lessons from Katchitavski.

I asked Daddy, and he looked mildly puzzled and said, "Punkin', doesn't that seem like a lot of money to spend for ten lessons, particularly when it's in Houston and you'd have to drive a hundred and twenty miles every day—there and back?"

"You're right, Dad." And I left the room. I didn't cry until I got to my room.

A minute later Mom came in. "Kathryn, I think it would be great fun for you to study with Katchitavski. Daddy and I can manage the money someway. We're not poor. And don't you worry about it, young lady. You're not supposed to make money now. Now you're supposed to get prepared for life, and if you get well prepared, when you do start making money, you'll make a lot more."

"You mean you don't think it's terribly selfish for me to want this now?"

"Honey, our Lord gives every human being some talents, and I think the selfish people are those who don't care enough about Him to develop those talents. That's the hardest thing, because developing talents takes time, and it takes a lot of work, and it takes a lot of money—sometimes when there's not much money to spare. But the selfishness—the sin—is wasting the talent our Lord gives us. Now, you think you're a pretty good dancer. Let's go see what Katchitavski thinks."

What started out to be two weeks of study turned out to be six —a lesson every day with the brilliant, patient little man who sat in a wicker rocker and tapped his cane on the floor. He thought my turnout was not very good, and advised me to stretch more. I went home and, assuming a frog's position, somehow managed to slide a trunk over my buttocks, and then went to sleep. Twenty minutes later I woke up paralyzed, and unable to get the huge burden off me. Old Pet, at her loudest, couldn't have bellowed louder than I did right then.

Mom and Frances Ruth came running up the stairs and when they finally stopped laughing, they removed the trunk and slowly, oh, so slowly, straightened out my legs. "You trying to go into a circus, Kathryn?"

"Oh, don't make fun. It hurts too much."

That autumn at TU college life was in full swing—football, rush week, even classes. Then there were my first tryouts for B. Iden Payne. Mr. Payne had directed *Dear Brutus* on Broadway when Helen Hayes made her debut, and now he was doing the same play again.

I read for the role of Margaret—and got it! The year was a whirl. Sometimes I had five Coke dates a day. Uncle Leon, driving through, took me for a date of his own and said, "Honey, I don't think you need to make straight A's. If you can make B's and have a good time too, that's fine. But I don't think you want to make any less than B's. And you're going to have to make a decision. Are you going to let your classes interfere with your dating?" Uncle twinkled. When he talked like that, there was no reason to rebel. He was right. I just cut down to one date a day.

Oh, things went so fast, and I found that I couldn't be successful in most areas of college life. I tried for Aqua Carnival Queen, and wasn't even second. A horrible bust.

Still, Austin was gay and exciting. There really wasn't much time to sit down and think—not even to talk to the others.

I learned during my final that you really have to take time off for this. I woke up feeling funny. Ruthie Munson, my roommate, was quietly stripping her bed. She'd been drenched during the night by some clever nonstudiers down the hall. She didn't say anything—just looked a little puzzled as she tried to dry out her mattress.

"When did it happen, Ruth?"

"About five minutes ago. What I'm wondering is when *you* happened."

"When I happened to what?" I started to sit up. Then I found out. I couldn't move. I was glued to the sheets with airplane glue. My waist-length hair was one solid hank of cement.

Ruth and I both tried to pull. It didn't work, so we took off the sheet, wrapped it around me like a turban cum sari, and marched down to the dorm counselor's room. She took one horrified look and put me in her tub, where the hot water did nothing but smear the mess around.

It had been such a great spring. Why, in Mr. Payne's production of *Much Ado About Nothing,* appendicitis overtook the chosen Hero and let me move up from playing a maid to the ingenue part —all in two hours. And Mr. Payne had come up to the dressing room and said, "You're a real trooper!" That had made the year a total success. If this veteran felt I was a trooper, there could be no question—I was bound for Broadway.

But here I was huddled up under a thoroughly ineffective faucet, knowing that when I got out I'd look like Mahatma Gandhi wearing a Medusa wig.

Well, in case you should ever find your head full of airplane glue, go directly to your nearest fingernail polish remover and apply liberally. This product will remove the glue—and also large hunks of hair. By the time they had finished with me, my waist-length Alice-in-Wonderland tresses were reduced to a prison cut.

The summer was full of confused combinations: a very short permanent, daily perusal of the history books for my postponed exam, and another bathing suit junket which left me Queen of the Texas Baseball League.

It was beginning to dawn on me that my life would not be a serene one. I felt as if I were on a nonstop roller coaster. All I could hope for was to be ready for the bumps when they came.

But I wasn't ready for what did happen. Maybe I should have noticed that Uncle Leon looked very thin, that his letters and Auntie's didn't come so frequently. That was all right. I was so bad at answering letters. Usually I just called collect.

Auntie began to sound a little preoccupied. And while I remembered Uncle was using a heat lamp for his bursitis the year before, I never thought it would be serious—not serious like cancer.

Uncle was buried in West Columbia near Grandma Stokely's grave.

I didn't want to go back to school. I didn't want to do anything but cry. Auntie snapped me out of it by saying, "Do you think your Uncle would want you to mope around like this? He talked your Dad into letting you major in Drama. Now you have a part in a play. You must go and do a good job of it."

"What are *you* going to do?"

"Do? I have to go back to school. I'm going to start teaching in Robstown next fall."

"But Auntie, you haven't taught school for twenty years."

Her chin lifted proudly. "You can do anything if you want to, Kathryn. Never forget that."

What I felt I had to do for Uncle was carry out our plans, our secret plans made so long ago. I worked very hard that spring, and actually won a role I coveted badly—the part of Isabel in *The Enchanted,* won it away from a consummate actress, Barbara Barry. She was a senior and I was just a sophomore, and she was kind enough to say, "Congratulations, you've been working hard. You deserve that." But I *had* to get there.

At the end of school my acting instructor said, "Look, Kathryn, we can't do anything with you here. Your mind is somewhere else —like maybe in California. Why don't you go out and give it a try?"

"You really think it's time?"

"I'll just say this, Kathryn. I had a chance to go out a long time ago. I turned it down because I didn't think I was ready. Now I'll never know."

I said good-bye to Dr. Winship, Dr. Payne—and fortunately kept my mouth shut this time. I could hardly announce: "And now I'm going out to Hollywood to set the town afire."

I looked at the familiar campus and thought, I'd really like to finish my education some day on these forty acres. Or maybe UCLA would be the answer.

Dad's Lion's Club asked me to represent them at the State Convention, so I put on my little white formal and became Queen of the Texas Lions. That was just the warm-up for the big one in Galveston, the Miss Texas contest.

I had been practicing quite a while for this. I had even found a reading in the college library, called "Letter to an Unborn Son":

> *My son sleeping now in the dark,*
> *Gathering strength for the struggle of birth . . .*

That would wow them at Galveston. They'd all be in tears. Then the judges would say, "Kathryn, after you are Miss America, you *must* go to Hollywood. There's never been such talent as yours. And we've been hearing about your great performances in *Henry's Hired Aunt* and *Dear Brutus*."

I would dimple modestly (why *wouldn't* both cheeks dimple?), ". . . and Nina Vance at Alley Theatre really wanted me to be Henrietta in *The Barretts of Wimpole Street!*"

Yes, that was the way it would go.

I was wearing my beautiful white formal. My mouth was dry, but I felt ready.

"Miss Kathryn Grandstaff of West Columbia."

I braced my shoulders and walked on stage. There was a little polite response from the crowd. Mom and Daddy were in the back of the audience, Leonard and Uncle Edgar down front. I took a deep breath, and began:

My son sleeping now in the dark . . .

The crowd had had a big dinner, and they had enjoyed the lively tap dance preceding my elocutionary gem. But gradually the rustling sounds and coughs died out, and before the five minutes were over and the piece was said, there was quiet and, when I had finished, warm response.

I left the stage confident that at least I'd done my best. A tall, beautiful blonde entered and told how she had made her own formal. I grimaced momentarily. Why hadn't Aunt Frances taught me how to sew? She could sew better than anyone in the whole world, and here I couldn't put on a button or tighten a snap.

I sat in the dressing room chatting lightly with the other girls, trying not to look, or be, tense. This was really the start of my whole career. If I was successful, Hollywood would be a cinch.

The five finalists were called. My name was the last. We marched back on the stage, curtsied, and walked off. Here it comes, I thought. The judge cleared his throat at the microphone and said, "Third runner up—Miss———. Second runner up—Miss———. First runner up—Miss Kathryn Grandstaff. Miss Texas—Miss Connie Hopping."

We walked on the stage. I assumed the cheerful, wan smile that I had seen Daddy's opponents wear after the election returns were counted.

So I wasn't Miss Texas. I'd failed. I'd failed Uncle. I'd failed the career that I'd wanted. Instead of Hollywood, I'd probably wind up teaching ballet in Robstown or West Columbia. Wild thoughts kept tumbling over and over in my mind. It wasn't what we had planned. All the plans had been . . .

I walked up to the tall, lovely blonde, the cool, regal beauty who had made her own formal. "Congratulations, Connie. You were so wonderful."

"Thank you." She smiled, exhibiting the great poise of the victor.

Well, it was over, done, finished. Nothing to do but pack up and go back to West Columbia.

I said a fond good-bye to two of the girls, and pretended to be busy until they left. Then I was all alone in the dressing room. I reread the wire from Emery, CONGRATULATIONS, MISS TEXAS—NEXT—MISS AMERICA. SIC 'EM, TIGER." Then I dissolved. I didn't cry or anything. I just sat there.

I heard heavy footsteps down the hall. It was probably Daddy coming to carry things out to the car. I looked at myself in the mirror. I almost laughed. The girl there had obviously undergone surgery, not just lost a silly old contest that really wasn't important anyway.

"Miss Grandstaff," the voice said.

I turned and dropped the overnight case. It was Bob O'Donnell. "Yes, sir."

"May I speak with you a minute?"

"Oh," I became unfrozen. "Please come in, sir. Sit down."

"You know, I think a contest like Miss America needs a tall blonde. They're more striking on a runway in Atlantic City."

I smiled, falsely, and a tiny nasty voice inside me said, "As a matter of fact, sir, I always fancied short, dumpy brunettes."

"Connie is lovely, isn't she?"

"Yes, she's very pretty."

"And talented—all that sewing. You don't sew, do you?"

"No, not a lick."

"I didn't think so. . . . You still interested in coming to Hollywood?"

The blood rushed to my cheeks. "Yes, sir."

"Well, you know, Kathryn, you really should try it. I think you might have a chance in films. You certainly have guts. The idea of reciting a tear-jerking letter to an unborn son to those festive merrymakers was brave, if nothing else."

I sat there with my smile quick-frozen again. I didn't know which way to turn now. Was I happy or miserable?

"Oh, Mr. O'Donnell. I'm so glad you came back tonight." Even as I spoke, quietly, politely, with my tea-party manners, the realization of what he had really said—what it really meant—kept stinging me like hot needles up and down my spine, and my ladylike decorum melted accordingly.

"Mr. O'Donnell, can I call Art Rush? I mean, if Dad would take me out to visit Aunt Ruth . . . she's his baby sister and lives in Topanga Canyon . . . you see, I met Art Rush when I was Miss Fat Stock—I mean Rodeo Queen of the Houston Fat Stock Show and Exposition—and I could go to Paramount on Monday, and probably test on Wednesday . . . and they'd sign me up—I mean, Dr. Payne said I'm ready. He's my acting teacher at the university."

My blood pressure had risen to the breaking point by then, and when Mom and Dad came in, I was hugging Mr. O'Donnell. "Mr. O'Donnell says I can go to Hollywood, even if I lost." Then there were hugs all around. Mr. O'Donnell shook his leonine head, and laughed a deep, satisfied laugh.

At this point Frances Ruth came in in tears. "It isn't fair; she should have won."

"Honey, forget it. Mr. O'Donnell says I ought to go to Hollywood."

CHAPTER 2

How To Marry Bing

Marriage should be so simple. You meet, fall in love, get married —just like that.

Well, my meeting with Bing was simple enough. It was a few months after I got to Hollywood. I had a big tennis date at UCLA, but first had to deliver a load of petticoats to Wardrobe at Paramount and on the way confer with Talent about a part. They had given me a test and I was under contract, but so far hadn't said a word or winked an eye about the silver screen. Nevertheless, I marched past Uncle Tom at the front desk looking like a delivery girl from the costume people.

"May I have your name? Oh, Kathryn. I could hardly see you behind those petticoats. You off to Milt Lewis?"

"Good morning, Tom. Right, but I have to hurry to Westwood for a tennis match after I take these to wardrobe. Gorgeous day, isn't it?"

I hurried past the fish pond and down dressing room row. Rosie Clooney's door was open and her Great Dane was sunning on the steps, but I guess she was shooting on Stage Nine.

Bing Crosby was standing in the doorway of his dressing room chatting with Barney Dean. I knew Barney was some special kind of writer called a gag man. Bing had just returned from Paris where he'd been on location for *Little Boy Lost*. I'd never met him.

"Howdy, Tex. What's your rush?"

"No rush, really," I said, skidding to a stop. "Hi, Barney, how are you?" I turned toward the man who had called me Tex and received full voltage from those robin's-egg-blue eyes. "No rush at all." I stood on one foot, dropped the tennis racket . . . picked it up. Two petticoats slid off my arm and were hastily retrieved.

"You look as if you needed to sit down for a spell. We're taking a little breather here while the company moves to another stage. Y'all shouldn't hurry so."

What was this? Was he teasing me about the Texas accent I was working so hard to lose? I looked again into those eyes—it didn't matter.

Barney and Mr. Crosby welcomed me to the shadowy interior of the dressing room. The glaring sun outside made this a cool haven. I parked the racket and tried to be poised about the petticoats—it wasn't as if they were falsies or wigs. Barney offered me a ginger ale, and while we sipped, the blond man near me explained the photo murals on the walls.

"Most of these are from the *Road* shows. Kathryn is your name, isn't it? Kathryn Grandstaff? And this is from *Going My Way* . . . *Bells of St. Mary's* over there . . ."

I knew.

"So you're a tennis player, eh? How good are you?"

My tennis match! Oh, dear. Well, if I dropped off the petticoats this evening or tomorrow . . .

"My brother and sister were fine players. I was a letterman at Robstown High, and I do love the game even though it's more agony than fun because I'm too short and fat to cover the court. But golf's your game, isn't it? Do you play much?"

"Just days." He smiled gently as his airy sally completely eluded me. He lit his pipe. "I play everywhere, every chance I get—here, Europe, Canada, Mexico, Palm Springs—all over. You know, between pictures, weekends—and of course the tournament is a big thing for me."

"Which one?"

"The Crosby in Pebble Beach."

"Oh."

There was an embarrassing silence. How could I be so insular?

Barney offered me some more ginger ale. "Thank you, no." Somewhat prissily.

"Well, do you like tea?"

"Yes, I love tea. I used to put a pot on the stove to simmer during final exams and just keep drinking. The stronger it got, the more history I could read."

"I wouldn't want to get all that pumped up, but our prop man, Jimmy, steeps some clover cambric every day about four P.M. Why don't you come by? Some days we feature macaroons."

"Tea's a good idea—but no macaroons for me. I'm on a diet. Oh, but I must go. Charlotte Clary said there might be a part for me in the next Martin and Lewis." I jumped up and grabbed my impedimenta.

"Good part?"

"Not with lines! I'll never get lines—not even in a Western shot in Texas. This time I'll be a manicurist, I think."

"Well, don't look in the lens!"

"Bye."

The next time we met, I was taking some visiting Texans over to the *White Christmas* set to watch Rosie Clooney, Bing, and Danny Kaye. A bicycle went by and stopped, and Bing said, "Hello, Tex." I introduced Gussie Glenn, a Chi Omega friend from Austin, and a real Southern belle. I was just the tiniest bit leary because . . . well, he was a very important star, and visiting with me when he had nothing better to do was one thing, but this was another.

He was charming to Gus, telling funny stories, entertaining her until he said, "Whoops—don't want to be late for work. Why don't y'all drop over after a while?"

Then, on the set, I sort of sensed someone to my left, and there was Bing. He brought up two chairs, and I sat by him—completely abandoning my awestruck companion to prop men, electricians, and wardrobe people. I didn't intend to be rude—it was just that all sanity had left me. Gus pretended to be engrossed with Danny Kaye's dialogue, but I'm sure her antennae were tuned backward to us. When we finally left Stage Nine, she started right out.

"He's just darlin', Kathryn. I declare he's the cutest, sweetest man I've ever seen. And have you ever in your life seen such blue eyes?"

No, I hadn't.

"Did you notice the way he looked at you?"

"No, I didn't." (Fat chance I'd tell *her* about my still racing pulse.)

"Doesn't he have gallant manners? He's the epitome, the very zenith of Southern charm."

"But he's from Washington."

"D.C.?"

"No—state."

Not too long after that I interviewed him on the set of *Country Girl.* I was doing a column, "Texas Girl in Hollywood," for twenty citizen newspapers down in Texas, and getting five dollars a week for it. I used to write it in twenty minutes and then zoom down to Publicity to borrow a special-delivery stamp so I could get it in on time.

Frank Riser from Publicity took me to the on-stage dressing room. I watched a scene from *Country Girl,* then during the break asked my questions.

"Mr. Crosby, because my readers live in ranch country, would you like to tell me a bit about your Elko ranch?"

"With or without drawl?" There was a glint which turned robin's-egg to sky-blue, and a half-smile. "Is Texas where you were for Christmas?"

"Yes, sir. Why?"

"Because I called your Topanga Canyon number and the man who answered said, 'So you're Bing Crosby; well, I'm Harry Truman,' and hung up on me."

"Oh, no! That's Uncle Walter Rasbury. I was staying with Daddy's sister Ruth, and I forgot to tell them you might call. But I can't blame Uncle Walter. When he and Aunt Ruth first moved to Hollywood, they took the lower half of a duplex. The first day there Uncle Walter went outside and his upstairs neighbor called down from the balcony, 'Hello there, neighbor; what's your name?'

" 'Rasbury. What's yours?'

" 'Broccoli.'

"Uncle Walter stared for a second, then stomped inside muttering, 'Smart Hollywood so-and-so.' " (This "smart Hollywood so-and-so" was Cubby Broccoli, later to bring James Bond to the screen.)

"But I'm so sorry. Uncle Walter is gruff but awfully nice once you get to know him . . . uh, maybe we better go on with the interview, Mr. Crosby."

Mr. Crosby gazed at me speculatively for a moment, one eyebrow raised quizzically. The girl reporter felt her poise dwindling.

"I think," he said sternly, "that these matters are serious enough to warrant development in depth, and to facilitate progress, why don't you call me Bing and I'll call you Kathryn. This interview can be continued over dinner for two—shall we say Sunday? I could pick you up at seven . . . but perhaps I'd better not drive out to Topanga Canyon—your uncle sounds a bit difficult."

"Not at all. But actually I live in Westwood now—11345 Berwick. I'll see you Sunday."

"Bye y'all."

The assistant director was waiting at the door. The publicity man walked me off the sound stage. "Honey," he said, "that's what I call getting a story."

I was living in a guest house in Westwood then, right next to UCLA. Mr. and Mrs. Charles Zibell had rented me the place for $30 a month, a very important budget item. And while they were solid citizens and worked for the United Jewish Appeal, they thought it was fun to have a "starlet" in the backyard, and they endured the inconvenience gamely. They even let me baby-sit with their little daughters, Naomi and Judy, after I settled in.

My guest cottage had red bougainvillaea all over the front porch. There was a fireplace in the corner made of gnarled bricks, bottles—even a ceramic Joan of Arc. There was a huge closet, just what I needed to hold all my clothes and then some. In the chest of drawers, the lingerie sometimes got mixed up with the ginger snaps; the peanut butter fell over on the small hot plate; but the desk with its student lamp was well placed, and there was a bed with a bedside stand. Of course there was no bathroom, but Mrs.

Zibell had given me permission to use the extra one at the back of their house.

Sunday, January 24, 1954, I was all over their house. Bing and I were going to Chasen's for dinner, and it was raining. Leah Zibell helped me as much as she could. She loaned me her pretty new black coat, which I wore over a burnt-orange taffeta dress I had bought at Sakowitz in Houston.

Leah had said I could meet him in their living room, instead of having him walk around to my cottage. So, when he arrived at seven, the Zibells were waiting to say good-evening. He seemed to approve of the way I looked as we climbed into the Mercedes and drove off to Chasen's, where we were greeted by the proprietor himself and ushered to the first booth on the right as you enter the small dining room. I'll admit I was thrilled—and scared.

He asked what I would like to drink. As a Texas Baptist, I had no real affinity or experience with liquor. He suggested a Dubonnet Mist, which sounded ethereal and wispy and harmless. But after two sips, I wished fervently that I'd had lunch. Then we had fresh cracked crab, a filet mignon, medium, a green salad, and later a frozen éclair. A heavenly dinner.

While we extricated the succulent crabmeat from the claws, we explored each other. So many unfamiliar horizons for me. Golf? I didn't know a tee from a green, really, though I had once garnered a trophy for being Junior Champion at the Robstown Country Club. I had a score of 85—for nine holes. My sole opponent had lost her ball and defaulted.

Bing was five times club champion at Lakeside; he had won the championships at Eldorado and Thunderbird. He had played in the United States, British, Italian, and French championships, and had won tournaments in Canada, South America, and Hawaii. He'd even made a hole in one seven times. So he had me there. Swimming? Bing had won seven medals in one meet in Spokane while the best I had ever done was to don a bathing suit and walk a runway at a beauty pageant, without mishap.

At this point I thought it wise to eschew sports altogether, so I segued into tours. Not so good. I'd made one to Korea. He'd been —well, he'd been all over the world. I took a swing into politics, rattling on about my father and his opinions, and a few half-baked ones of my own. This brought an amused sort of a gleam to his eye, and a half-smile to his lips. I later learned to translate this as, "Women are such charming idiots; we must humor them." I tried a few other gambits and ploys, threw up a few trial balloons—art, music, literature. He topped me on everything.

By the time we'd finished the *filet de boeuf,* I became possessed of a new feeling, a new perception. Not infatuation, and certainly not love at first sight, but something different: a startling realization that this was a man—a man who knew a lot, understood more, and had accomplished much. No matter what I might do, it would be nothing beside his achievements. Yet he wasn't at all self-satisfied. Always he remained a man of imagination and sly good humor. I choked on my after-dinner coffee thinking of all this, and the choking was just one more thing to laugh about.

On the drive home, the rain had ceased; the stars vied with the lights of Beverly Hills and Westwood. Bing hummed a few bars, then started, "Sometimes I'm happy . . ." I threw in some harmony, and our first duet was sung. Then he took my hand and sang, "You'd Be So Easy to Love," and my toes went numb. That was new, too. Curiously, I'd never had numb toes before. When we arrived at the Zibell's, he didn't come in. He took me to the door, looked at me a minute with those blue eyes, and said goodnight.

Next morning the mail brought me several unpleasant shocks. Paramount had dropped my option. The Citizens Newspapers had dropped my column. UCLA had dropped me from the Drama Department.

I wrote a long letter home, then took a long look at myself. It was evident I had a new title: "Miss Most-Dropped of 1954."

Off to UCLA, where the counselor said I might continue with electives: Interior Design, Political Science, Cooking. I needed them all and accepted her suggestion with alacrity, realizing that the cooking class would save my buying lunch. If Bing would ask me out to supper once in a while, I could somehow survive even on my income.

In fact, most of the dates before Bing's proposal were quiet dinners. Maybe he thought I wasn't eating properly? Then one day at school I made a cheesecake. It was exquisite, so I dropped off a note at Paramount saying I needed a customer to try my masterpiece. Bing responded with yet another invitation to dinner, but even I wasn't bold enough to lug my cake into Romanoff's. We came home to eat it later. In fact, he had seconds, after which he quietly mused, "You know, Kathy, I think I'm going to have to ask you a question one of these days—when I know what the answer is."

Yes, I thought. Well?

Then he put his pipe in his jacket and went home. But I noticed he hadn't knocked the ashes out of the pipe before leaving.

After that our dates were casual for a while and sort of few and far between, but our friendship was kept going by correspondence. Oh, I can't say our letters equaled those of George Bernard Shaw and Ellen Terry. They were sort of cursory weather reports, mixed with sports news and trivia. At this point I hadn't much to write about. I was too busy thinking of in-come and out-go.

I went to Columbia Pictures with my new agent, Mel Shauer, to see if I could get a contract there. Max Arnow was the head of Talent, and took me to see Harry Cohn, the President.

Now I had met other studio heads, like Y. Frank Freeman from Paramount. He was gentle, with gracious manners, and not at all like Harry Cohn, who was famous for his temper and rudeness. Nobody in the world was like Harry Cohn. I'll never forget that first meeting. I walked into his office and was agape. Behind the desk was a sideboard full of Oscars. A pile of scripts was on his left, papers on his right. The phones were going—sometimes two and three at a time. He was talking when I entered with Mr. Arnow, and he waved me to sit down—imperiously, I thought.

I fluttered into a chair and waited, and waited, and *waited*. I could feel my temperature rising, and my security dissolving. After what seemed an hour he hung up, turned to me, and asked a few abrupt questions. I answered him as well as I could, but within my heart of hearts I knew the whole thing was a horrible mistake.

I didn't want to be under contract to Columbia. I just wanted to get out of the studio alive. I had missed breakfast and I wanted a package of raisins right then—Sun Maid raisins with the little girl smiling on the top of the red box, so safe and secure.

"No, Mr. Cohn, I have never had a lead in a picture. My part in *The Unchained* was a very small part, but it did have dramatic possibilities—at least that's what they told me. . . . No, Mr. Cohn, in my year and a half at Paramount I did not have a speaking part in a film unless you count the two words that were left in *Arrowhead,* which were 'Oh, Daddy.' . . . Yes, Mr. Cohn, I do think I have some talent. . . . How can I prove it? Well, there's no recent film of me—none that I could get, anyway."

Harry Cohn turned to Mr. Arnow and said, "About her salary. We won't kick her upstairs, but we won't kick her downstairs either."

Now what did he mean by that? Who was going to kick whom? Nobody was going to kick me! I rose, with dignity, I hoped, and left the office. I didn't go back to Mr. Arnow's office. I turned my head neither to the right nor to the left until I was out the studio gate and back in my car—the little Ford I had won for being Miss Fat Stock.

I stopped off at Mel Shauer's and he asked, "Well, how did it go?"

I was quivering, I was so mad, and I replied as plainly as I could, "He didn't like me, but I couldn't stand him either; so we're quits."

Mel tried to soothe me. He gave me a large glass of lemonade, and then the phone rang. Mr. Arnow's secretary, Virginia Smith, asked, "Where are you? We've been looking for you for the last twenty minutes. Here's Mr. Arnow."

Mr. Arnow said, "You're a bit of a Texas spitfire, aren't you? What Mr. Cohn meant was that you wouldn't get a raise, but that you wouldn't get a cut in salary either. We'd like to do a screen test. Is that all right with Miss Buccaneer?"

I had to giggle. I was delighted that they wanted to do a screen test.

A scene from *Picnic* was chosen, and Benno Schneider got us ready for the test. I worked with a boy named Vince Edwards and another one named Kerwin Matthews. We all tested the same day, with Danny Taradash directing. When the day was over, we all went across the street to a little restaurant called Naples where we toasted each other, toasted the hope that we'd come off well, and toasted Mr. Taradash. Then we went our separate ways to wait and pray.

Waiting was ghastly. To keep calm, I decided to take the varnish off the bedside stand. Nobody ever told me that varnish removers have to be handled carefully or they'll coat your fingers permanently. For days my hands looked like a mummy's.

Then finally Mr. Arnow called and said, "We want you under contract to Columbia."

"That's great, Mr. Arnow, but will it be possible to go on with school? I'm getting toward the degree, and I'd hate to stop now."

Mr. Arnow said, "We'll take care of that. Dr. Barkley will help you."

Lillian Barkley was the head of education on the lot. She had been Shirley Temple's schoolteacher. How can I describe her?

She was a little woman, terribly thin. Neither old nor young, her eyes were brown and deep—sympathetic, comforting, giving, inspiring. Her jaw could get very firm on occasion; but her voice was the thing. Her voice expressed her mind perfectly. It was completely objective, like her viewpoint.

Max told me she had brought children that were a year behind in their studies to be right up with their regular classes when they returned to public school—and while they held full-time acting jobs.

She tutored me through the last year at the University of Texas, working with Dr. Winship and Dean Doty so I could finish the college work in a single summer on campus.

Later, much later, she started me on my work at Queen of Angels, introducing me to Dr. Gallant and all the people down at the hospital. And she helped me to earn my teaching credentials. All these things she does for so many people in her schoolroom, a small canvas square, just four flats thrown together on Stage 1 at Columbia.

Mornings then were devoted to Benno Schneider, the Drama coach. Kerwin Matthews and I hit it off very well right from the test, so we'd come in and work together at eight each morning, and by the time Benno got there at ten we were ready to do a scene.

He watched us for about three weeks, and then one day he very cautiously said, "I think you're both going to be all right. If you can keep on working like this, you'll succeed."

Benno was a fascinating man, a very gentle personality. He'd studied with Stanislavsky, not only in Russia, but when the great stage director toured the United States. He told us many stories of working with his teacher.

One day Benno rode home with him after rehearsal. Naturally reticent, that night Benno was even quieter than usual. Finally Stanislavsky said, "You're very quiet tonight. What's troubling you?"

He responded, "Well, sir, I went to a small amateur production yesterday. There was a young girl, only sixteen. She knew nothing of The Method. She knew nothing of technique. Her body was awkward, and yet I could not take my eyes off her. Every word she said I listened to eagerly, and I believed it with all my heart."

"Ah," said the Maestro, "perhaps she had *talent.*"

Benno tried hard to bring any talent we had to the surface. He thought that acting was not merely learning artificial techniques, but stripping artifice until the real personality was reached. I think if he'd been any tougher, he couldn't have worked with us so intensively, but his very gentleness allowed him to be cruel, to demand our best.

When I signed, the other girls under contract were Kim Novak, Jana Mason, Adele August, Gloria Krieger, Felicia Farr, and Lucy Marlow. We used to call ourselves the Class of Fifty-four at Columbia U. Each one of us cheered the others on. We were all, I think, delighted when any of us got any kind of break.

Bing and I celebrated my new contract by going to a football game. We were the guests of Dave Butler, the film director and rabid sports fan. Bing said he was the loudest rooter since Foghorn Murphy. When Butler's team was winning, he could be heard for miles around.

This particular game was a championship contest between the Cleveland Browns and the Los Angeles Rams, and Cleveland had sent out a delegation of loyal rooters—two hundred strong—to witness the competition. They sat directly in front of us while the Rams made a runaway of the contest, scoring four touchdowns in the first half. All through the game Dave carried on lustily, crying, "Oh, you Rams, I love you Rams. Let's get one more, Rams." The Cleveland rooters squirmed in their seats, looking over their shoulders disgustedly, until finally one of them rose and shouted at Dave, "Why don't you shut up? You and your damn Rams."

Dave drew himself up to his full height—all two hundred and eighty pounds and six feet four of him, and said, "But, sir, I went to Ram."

The next step after getting my career back on the rails was to find a place to live closer to the Columbia studio. It made no sense to live near UCLA any longer since I was going back to the University of Texas to get my degree. So, with Aunt Mary's permission, I shared an apartment with her daughter Marilyn.

We found a tiny little place in the San Fernando Valley. I remember the housewarming dinner I cooked for Bing. The shrimp cocktails were all right—just boil and drown in catsup and serve. But when I got to the leg of the lamb, I kept calling Aunt Mary every five minutes, asking, "What do I do with it now?" Then I put salad dressing on the romaine two hours early. Poor Bing. How brave he was to try to eat it. It was limp and slimy—and tasted the same way. He just said it seemed a bit tired, as if it had the vapors.

There was an awkward moment because I had no ash trays. I didn't smoke and was trying to break Marilyn of the habit, so I had hidden all possible receptacles. When I finally caught Bing putting ashes in his trouser cuff, I had to bring out a saucer. He couldn't have been more polite about it, blandly commenting "not to worry. It keeps the moths away."

His real proposal came on October 30. Marilyn and I were invited to visit him in Palm Springs. That evening we sat by the pool watching the stars and listening to some romantic music. He had told me when he invited me that he wanted to talk to me about something rather serious, so Marilyn retired immediately after supper. I did think she looked rather ludicrous sneaking in, clad in yellow pajamas, to change the records from time to time, but both Bing and I pretended not to notice. Her choice of records seemed a little obvious—"I'm in the Mood for Love" and Jackie Gleason orchestral arrangements with strings galore.

Bing didn't seem romantically inclined. He just seemed worried. He must have been aware of lots of things of which I was ignorant—problems we would have to face, public relations, good and bad—that we would have to overcome. He didn't discuss such things with me then, but he did seem a bit withdrawn for a man who was figuratively on his knees requesting my hand in marriage.

When he had first said, "I have a question to ask you when I know what the answer is going to be," I don't remember what I said or did, aside from simpering, but I think it was something about roots. I've always had a very strong feeling about friendship. I thought originally we needed lots and lots of time to get to know each other better, to let our friendship grow deeper. But at heart I knew that our friendship was quite deep enough. By the time Bing did propose, I felt that the roots had grown very strong, that we were really close, and that our bond of understanding was valid.

I still knew little about Bing the great star, the idol of millions. I did know a great deal about a very kind man who seemed to enjoy my company, as I enjoyed his. I'd met many other stars. Charlton Heston was on the Paramount lot when I was first there, and I thought he was the biggest movie star I'd ever seen—literally. He looked about six feet eight inches tall, and lanky with a big flashy smile. He almost scared me to death. Then I had done my screen test with William Holden. He was very kind, but he was also very smooth and cultivated and sophisticated. He made me stutter, even during my screen test.

Bing never made me stutter. Bing made me speak more clearly than ever before in my life. He listened to my few opinions with interest and acceptance. He seemed to think I knew what I was talking about, and he showed me he was proud of my endeavors and of my activities. Of course I liked that. I liked that enough to want to be with him the rest of my life, and I was delighted when he said he felt the same way.

But now he discussed plans for the years that were to come for him, and speculated on how I might fit in with those plans. Just as he was saying, "You mean you might want to marry me?" and I was replying rather casually, I thought, "Yes, I believe so," just at that very crucial moment, out came Marilyn, crawling on her hands and knees in those yellow pajamas to change the record. A Benno Schneider couldn't have staged it better. We both broke up laughing, turned off the record player, and Marilyn and I went off to our end of the house. When I threatened cheerfully to kill my little roommate, she protested, "I was just doing what I could to help, Kathryn."

A wedding date was set, but before then several things occurred. I went to Europe on a USO tour for the Christmas season and came back to find that Bing was very ill with a kidney stone attack. That was a ghastly time. He was in Pebble Beach and I was in Hollywood doing a Ford Theatre show for television. The only reason I didn't ditch it and go to Pebble was that he kept pleading with me not to come. I thought at the time he was just trying to be thoughtful, but now I realize he would have hated me there.

When he did recover, he asked me to go to the Academy Awards with him. What an evening that was! Leo Lynn picked me up at the Make-up Department at Columbia, and then we got Bing from his dressing room at Paramount. (Leo was always picking me up for some exciting event.) Bing was nominated for an Oscar for his *Country Girl* performance, and so was Grace Kelly. As we walked into the theater, all the publicity people saw us, of course, and the fans leaned over the car, calling, "There's Bing Crosby. Isn't he wonderful?" There were a few murmurs of "Who's she?"

We sat on the aisle and the tension was terrific until the judge's decision was announced. Yet Bing was perfectly calm, and when Marlon Brando was named for his acting in *On the Waterfront,* Bing, who normally moves rather slowly, turned in a flash to shake his hand and congratulate him with obvious sincerity. And Grace Kelly did win. Bing was very proud of her. I was furious that Bing hadn't won, but he didn't seem to mind at all.

The party afterward was gorgeous. We danced and talked, and I enjoyed all the flurry over our appearance together. But later, when Bing took me home, he said very somberly, "Things won't be the same now, you know. We're an 'item.' "

"Why should they be the same?" I was going to Phoenix City next morning to play my first starring role in a movie, and the Academy Award night seemed like a dream—a Cinderella's ball. Everything wonderful was beginning. Why should things always be the same?

But Bing was right. It hadn't occurred to me until the month after the Awards that Bing was public property in a way, and that he respected his obligation to the public.

After *Phoenix City Story* I went back to Texas to finish up my studies. Mother was my roommate at the university for six weeks, and between classes we worked on arrangements for a September wedding.

This wasn't the first time we had a definite wedding date—or the last. In fact, I was to become so used to wedding dates that I'd wake up in the mornings and have to think before doing anything else, "Is this a wedding day or not?" The first was the seventh of February. I was going to marry Bing in Carmel, and Aunt Mary was going to be matron of honor, and Mother and Dad were going to fly out quietly, and the ceremony would be at the old Mission where Junípero Serra is buried. What a beautiful plan that was. Well, that was when the kidney stone broke loose and wrecked everything.

Then, about the time of the Academy Awards, I was going to be a spring bride, on the second of May. That's when the movie lead intervened. Now came the third date, September 10. I was ready. I'd finished my college career. I had played the lead in one film, and done a public appearance tour for the studio. They seemed very happy about me at Columbia. My family, Mother and Dad, were content with my future, and I was about to embark on a great adventure—marriage to the man I loved. What could be more perfect?

Yet on the way up to Hayden Lake, where we were going to be married this time, I felt my usually warm feet getting very, very cold. Something was decidedly wrong with my circulation. I thought at the time it was just the plane's altitude.

I'll always remember the third of September, to paraphrase the Tom Jones and Harvey Schmidt song. Bing met me at the airport.

He was very gay, and said with a welcoming warmth, "I'm not going to let you go home this time. You've traipsed around enough."

Of course I think he said this before he took a second look at me. I was green from the bumpy landing and had dark circles under my eyes from those late nights of study at Texas. But we drove on to Hayden Lake, Bing telling me about his friend, Father Francis Corkery, the Jesuit he had known ever since they were children. Father Corkery was going to marry us, and was waiting to give me instruction about the wedding.

We arrived at Bing's new home, right on Hayden Lake, and there I met Mary Henderson, a Georgia girl who was dating Bing's writer, Bill Morrow. Mary was going to be my maid of honor at the secret wedding. She told me several months later that she knew we'd get along by the independent way I carried my own luggage into the house. I liked her immediately. She had a Southern drawl, and dark brown hair and melting brown eyes.

During the next few days Mary and I became good friends. We learned to water-ski. We got to know Bing's son Lindsay and his girl better. And I learned a lot of important things. I guess any courtship needs a situation like our first stay at Hayden Lake—a sort of cooling-off period for both of us.

I learned more about why I loved Bing. He took me to the church in Spokane so I could receive instruction from Father Corkery, and showed me the sacristy where there was a statue of St. Joseph. "I got one of my worst lickings because of that statue," he said.

"Why, Bing? Why would you ever be punished because you were praying to a Saint?"

"It wasn't praying, Kathryn. You see, I put a baseball suit on him because our team was playing a very important game, and I thought he'd help by wearing our uniform—all but the shoes."

"Scandalous!"

"Yes, Mother thought so."

Bing and I drove around the house where he had lived as a boy. A white house, not unlike the one I grew up in, but with a steep roof to shed the snow. There were no pecan trees in the yard, just pines and cedars. It seemed a bit severe and Spartan to me.

His papers didn't come in from Tacoma, and while he was waiting for his mother's reply to a letter he'd written asking her blessing, I risked making some candy—a very bad move. I made divinity, which was a moderate success, and butterscotch toffee, which was not. We couldn't even get it out of the pan and had to throw the whole thing in the lake. The fish in that area must have had a high blood-sugar content for days.

Bing and I took the little motorboat on a trip across the lake, and got stuck right in the middle because we ran out of gas. It was a long, long row to either bank. Bing rowed and I dragged my hand in the water like a Victorian lady punting on the Thames. We finally made the shore, where a man who had been watching us asked archly, "Out of gas?" Bing filled up the empty tank and eventually we put-putted back home.

On the third day I began to feel I wasn't ready to get married. No, my Bachelor of Fine Arts from Texas was only the beginning of knowledge. Instead of wedding cake, Bing and I ate a large amount of ham and chicken on rye, and developed some kind of mental telepathy, for when one morning I said, "Bing, I think I'd better get back to the studio now," he answered without a trace of surprise, "Fine, dear, I'll take you back."

Mary and Bill were terribly confused. But I knew I was doing the right thing. I needed to grow up before I could tackle any more changes in my life. And I was intellectually exhausted. The six weeks in Texas had really done me in, for I had experienced not only mental growth but a complete spiritual change.

I had become a Catholic that summer. My six weeks of intensive study with Father Murphy at the Newman Center at the University of Texas had opened a whole new world to me—a full and exciting one.

Bing had never suggested I join his church, nor had I ever considered it. I had been very happy in California as a Methodist when I found there was no Baptist church like the one at home for me to attend. I'd gone to the Methodist church often with Aunt Frances and Uncle Leon in the valley, so I simply continued going there. But then Dr. Theodore Palmquist was moved to Washington, and I began to travel so much that I felt it was time to join a church I could attend every Sunday.

That summer in Austin Mother went with me to Dr. Blake Smith, the Baptist preacher who had been such a good friend when I first studied at the university. "Dr. Smith, I'm looking for a good priest. I want to become a Catholic."

"Why, Kathryn?"

"Well, it's something that happened very suddenly, Dr. Smith. We made a USO tour last Christmas in France. We went to twenty-one bases in twenty-one days, and on Christmas Day we were in Paris and I went to Mass at Sacré Coeur. I travel so much now, Dr. Smith, I can't find a Baptist church everywhere, but I do need faith. I need to be able to worship. And that Christmas morning I heard the most beautiful music, and I found myself kneeling with hundreds and hundreds of people and I felt very much at home on that hard wooden kneeler."

"Well, Kathryn, Father Murphy here is a fine priest. See him, but you'll keep in touch, won't you?"

Father Murphy was a fine priest indeed, a Paulist at the Newman Center, and Mother and I went together to the first two meetings. After the third day Mother decided that I was going to be all right, so she stayed home. Father Murphy said, "Please tell your mother we miss her."

Poor Mother. Strict Baptist that she was, she went through the entire course of instruction with me, and toward the very last she said, "You know, Kathryn, you aren't learning anything different from the things we've always taught you. You've just learned a lot more."

Oh, and that day of decision when Father Murphy said, "I think you'd better wait a while, Kathryn. Give it more consideration and then, after six months or so, come back to me and tell me what you think."

Mother seconded, "Yes, I think you'd better wait too, Kathryn. You've had only six weeks of instruction."

I looked at both of them, the sillies, and said, "But you can't keep me out. I have a right to be a member of the Church."

Father Murphy smiled, "You're right, Kathryn, we can't keep you out."

Mother couldn't help looking a little distressed, and then she said, "Well, as long as you go to church every Sunday and keep on reading your Bible, I think it's fine."

My father and Frances Ruth came up from West Columbia, and Mother and I were all excited about my baptism. I'd taken my last exam for the college degree that day, and Dr. Winship had assured me that I would pass. "I don't think either one of us could take any more of this kind of pressure," he said.

That evening I dressed in my demure black dress, and the Grandstaffs went to the Catholic church. Daddy looked a bit solemn as we entered. After all, he'd been a Mason for years, but the ceiling didn't fall in. We went into the baptistry and Father Murphy baptized me with the oils and the Latin and the burning of candles and incense. After I had received the sacrament of baptism, I went into the confessional and received the sacrament of penance. Then we all went up to the rail to take part in the conversion ceremony, and I received my First Communion.

I was filled to overflowing. Mother was weeping—she always weeps when she is happy. My sister looked terribly impressed. And Daddy still looked quite solemn.

Finally the service was over. We said good-bye to Father Murphy and I went out into the night. I really felt as if I were sprouting wings. I turned to my father and said, "Daddy, what did you think of it?"

He looked at me quizzically, and said with quiet finality, "It looked like a dad-gummed Inca ceremony."

Mom and I began to laugh hysterically. After our six weeks of instruction, we just assumed that everyone would be impressed. But Protestant America has one staunch holdout. Daddy will never budge.

Next day he relented slightly and mused wryly, "Well, Kathryn, you've been dipped, sprinkled, and poured. If there's *any* way to get to heaven, I think you're going to make it."

Yet I still wasn't sure about marriage. Bing might have genius in his vocal chords, but he was not mechanically inclined. (I thought, quite unfairly, of that nonfunctioning motorboat.) No, Hayden Lake might be all right for him. Hollywood for me, who- ever I was. Each new role revealed new facets.

Storm Center taught me what a fine actress like Bette Davis can do. *The Wild Party* made me a way-out beatnik for a few weeks. In *Reprisal* I was a Mascalero Apache. In *Guns of Fort Petticoat* I got thrown over Audie Murphy's head with the wicked- est bit of sleight of hand that Audie and George Marshall could concoct.

I found out more about who I was in a delightful film called *Mister Cory,* where I shot pool with Tony Curtis. That was fun.

After *Mister Cory,* I took a vacation from the studio. I flew up to meet Mom and Dad and Aunt Frances in Seattle, and they all met Bing for the first time.

I was nervous as a gnat. I wanted Mom and Dad to approve of Bing. And, strangely, I wondered if they would. It really didn't matter that the whole world loved Bing. If Mom and Dad didn't like him, I knew they wouldn't pretend. Of course they'd never let him know. They were too kind for that, and they'd never say so to me, so I kept looking for little signs, little clues. Pretty soon Daddy relaxed. I think it was just after Bing described to him his first hunting encounter with a Rocky Mountain sheep, after a four-day stalk in Canada. Daddy related some of his own exploits, the spawning cycle of the salmon was discussed and marveled at, and we ladies listened with polite interest. When an opening appeared, Auntie said brightly, "I bet Bing would like my German chocolate cake."

"I'd love it for tea, Frances. Hope you'll make me one some day." Obviously all was well.

Then, in 1956, we made our second trip to Hayden Lake. Mar- riage should be simplicity. Hateful Hayden. Again it all became much too complex and for the second time I found I couldn't go through with it.

I'd told Mother and Aunt Mary that I was going up to Hayden. Aunt Mary said, "I don't think you should do this, Kathryn." And I said, "But Aunt Mary, it's definite this time. The church is all arranged. I've all my papers. We won't have to worry about waiting for the banns or anything. We'll be calling you the second the ceremony is over."

At the little airport in Spokane, Bing showed Mary Morrow and me the evening paper. There had been a press leak when Bing had asked for his baptismal certificate. And in Dorothy Kilgallen's column was the item: "It has to be serious. They stopped at a restaurant and she opened the car door for herself."

Bing went to take part in ground-breaking ceremonies for the Crosby Library at Gonzaga University. He shoveled the dirt for the press photographers, and there were speakers. While this was going on, I was sneaking in for more instruction at St. Aloysius. Suddenly mail and clippings started to arrive in profusion, and we made the gross error of reading them. Most letters came from well-meaning people who seemed to feel that Bing had no right to marry again after having had such a beautiful wife as Dixie Lee for so many years. Perhaps they felt his four sons would require all his attention. Some women writers were outraged because they had loved Bing very much for years and felt I was an interloper trying to steal their precious idol. What could I say? He was precious, all right, but I had no intention of monopolizing him—at least not professionally. I felt our marriage would bring a new lilt to his songs.

There was humor of a sort. One morning the newsmen set up batteries of cameras on the front lawn to photograph the house. Visualizing captions like "Crosby Love Nest," Bing flung up the window shouting imprecations and ordering them to leave the premises. They all fled, but one, less timorous than the others, called out, "Where's Kathryn Grant?" Bing yelled back, "I hear she's on a pack trip up the Bitterroot Mountains." I told him he looked like Barbara Frietchie, "Shoot if you must this old gray head," and all that.

But it did no good to laugh about it all. The problem remained. The day of the wedding, September 10, Father Corkery called. The church was full of reporters, television cameras, the whole works —and Bing had left his hairpiece in Hollywood!

We just didn't feel like running the gauntlet. Why did life have to be so complicated? Why had I stood up that tennis date so long ago?

Bing breathed a weary sigh. "Father Corkery and I talked at great length today. Kathryn, maybe we are wrong. Maybe the world is trying to tell us something."

I looked at him with rather glazed eyes and said, "Could we go down to the boathouse and talk?" The boathouse was the only place where there was any semblance of privacy. Bill and Mary Morrow, who were Mr. and Mrs. now, Lemon, the plump, jolly cook, and the housekeeper were all here, nice but ubiquitous. There really wasn't any other place for heart-to-heart talks. He nodded soberly and off we trudged.

There were no laugh crinkles in the corners of his eyes now. He looked drawn and unhappy. I must have looked particularly woebegone and mousy. And a curiously uncomfortable feeling was coming over me—a haunted feeling, almost a hunted feeling.

When we were uncomfortably seated in the launch—the outboard that had let us down the year before—I said, "Bing, I might go home now, but if I do, I won't see you anymore. If we're not supposed to be married, then we're not; but this is enough. I've had it. This situation is like the time we were stranded in the middle of the lake with no gasoline—we couldn't go forward and we couldn't go back. We were drifting. It's just not fair. It's just not right. I'll go home content if you will only tell me you don't love me. That's all I ask."

I expected him to say, "Well, Kathryn, perhaps you are too young for me, like everyone says." Or, "No, Kathryn, I guess I don't love you. You're just little Kathy Grant to me, a nice tomato from Texas."

Instead he said, "I love you and I always will."

I felt terribly confused and wanted to get away to think it over. So I asked him to take me to the plane, right then, fifty miles away in Spokane. It was pretty impractical, but I've always been impractical. He said, "I'll tell you what. You and Mary go to bed now and in the morning I'll take you to the plane."

I was furious. I yelled at him. "If I stay tonight, I'll stay until the bitter end, and you'll have to work something out." He looked so uncomfortable and so miserable, poor angel. Poor angel? Here I was feeling sorry for him. Why didn't I think about myself for a minute? All I'd done was burn every bridge behind me!

I'd given up my apartment with Marilyn. I'd turned down a job for TV from Columbia Pictures, which might mean I was suspended or fired. I was a disaster area.

I did stay the night, and next morning he'd worked something out. Something of a sort, at least. We were to drive to the ranch at Rising River. He'd scheduled a hospital benefit at Fall River Mills, a community near there. He would do the show, which would divert the hue and cry for a bit, and then we'd slip over to Las Vegas, where we could be married without the necessity of the usual three-day waiting period. I'd waited three years. What was three days?

So we set out for northern California, Mary and I spelling Bing at the wheel. Bill Morrow, Leo Lynn, and much of the impedimenta came in the next car. Quite a cavalcade we were, and the press didn't leave us.

Bing did the show, and Mary and I lashed Rising River to a froth trying to learn how to throw a dry fly. Bing then called Las Vegas and learned from friends that there were newsmen lurking about. They seemed to have divined our intentions. But, after all, what were we fleeing from? A good question. Was it procrastination? Or was Bing, as he averred, loath to have our wedding turned into a carnival?

We seemed to be constantly retreating to previously prepared positions. Instead of Las Vegas the next day, off we went, a very travel-weary little wedding party, to Pebble Beach, where Bing had promised to do a television show. We all moved into his new house, where I found for the first time that I was embarrassed about meeting people. By this time it really didn't matter that Bing said we'd fly somewhere to be married right after the television show was finished. I was beginning to feel that I had my answer.

It was very simple. Love without responsibilities is not love, and Bing and I were both being more responsible to the public, to the press, to the mysterious "they" out there, than we were to each other.

The morning after the TV show was filmed, Bing went to play golf, and I took a long walk along the ocean. Pebble Beach is an absolutely magnificent place to think. There is a cool, fresh breeze, and lots of sand for bare feet, and lots of rocks to climb over. As I meandered along, the events of the past few years began to come into focus.

Then a lovely thing happened. A sailor on the beach whistled at me, and I smiled. He didn't know who I was, and couldn't have cared less. But I was still free, and something told me I ought to stay that way. This didn't mean that I didn't love Bing, but I was through worrying about churches full of photographers and letters from well-meaning strangers, friendly or hostile. I thought of another very important item—the pain I must be giving my family. My decision was made: The courtship was finished.

I walked along the beach to the mission—almost five miles— then slowly back again. By the time I reached Bing's house, I was quite calm. Bing, for him, was frantic. He even lifted his eyebrows a bit. I think he thought I might have thrown myself into the ocean or something stupid. But not a chance. I was almost gay as I packed, and when I came down, I said quietly, because that was the way we communicated, "Bing, I have to go back to Los Angeles for a while. There are some things I want to settle." (Where was I going to live? Was I still under contract after refusing that Ford Theatre show without reason? You know, little items like that . . .) He looked fairly bland and merely said, "Fine, dear."

I went upstairs and called Hollywood. Mr. Cohn spoke to me. "Mr. Cohn, I'm coming home."

"Very well, Miss Grant. Come right to my office from the airport."

"Yes, sir. And Mr. Cohn, am I still working for you?"

"Of course. I'll see you in the morning."

"Thank you, sir."

All right, I had a job. The next problem: a place to live. I couldn't call Aunt Mary. She was the one who had told me the wedding wouldn't work out. I couldn't face her—not yet.

Where could I go? Nancy Quinn? My little stand-in, my friend who'd made so many orange flips for me in the mornings when we'd gone off on location to shoot *Reprisal* and *Guns of Fort Petticoat,* and even *Mister Cory.* Yes, Nancy would be kind.

I called her home. Her dad, Don Quinn, creator of *Fibber Mc-Gee and Molly* and *Halls of Ivy,* answered. "Mr. Quinn, I'd like to come and stay with Nancy, if she's there."

"She's in Hawaii, Princess, but you're welcome as the flowers in May. Edith and I will do our best to take care of you." His voice was warm.

"Thank you, Mr. Quinn." Welcome as the flowers in May— that's how he made me feel.

The last supper at Pebble Beach was a rather strained occasion. I didn't have much to say, though I tried to be pleasant and light, and so did everyone else. Poor Mary looked dreadfully upset, and Bill's quips fell flat. Bing said nothing.

Next morning I was off to the airport. Bing went to play golf. "I'll call you in a few days, Kathryn. Have a nice trip." A good-bye peck on the cheek.

"Wonderful—call me." But I knew he wouldn't call, and if he did, he wouldn't reach me—not anymore. Not ever, ever again!

I couldn't believe Mr. Cohn's reaction when I got to the studio. I was ushered immediately into his office, and here was this man who had refused to let me be in *Eighty Days Around the World* because he was mad at Mike Todd. Here was the man who'd said, "I wouldn't kick you upstairs, or downstairs, either." He stood up, came around the desk, took my hand, and said, "Miss Grant, how may I help you?"

I suddenly strangled on the lump that came in my throat. I think I'd have liked it better if he'd yelled at me, or been mean or mad. But this courtesy was almost too much. I blurted out, "I'd like to go to work."

"All right, dear. Here are three scripts. Read them and let's see when we can get started."

After a day or two, I finally got up nerve to call Aunt Mary. She just said, "Honey, we're having spoonbread and fried chicken for supper. We'll see you at six."

Then we went hunting for an apartment, and found one right next door to El Camino Drive. Now I was a bachelor girl who meant to stay that way. The landlord gave me close appraising looks, and then looked at Aunt Mary and her firm jaw and said, "Very well, Miss Grant, we'd love to have you."

At first it was sort of like recovering from an amputation. I wanted no sympathy, and thank heaven I received none. Aunt Mary never said a word. Neither did anyone at the studio.

Mr. Arnow said, "There's a USO tour coming up. Would you like to go?"

"Please." This would be the third one for me.

They threw me into bit parts at the studio. Anything to keep me busy. I played an Italian woman in *Brothers Rico,* and Phil Carlson let me do my part in two days and worked the crew late so I could get off to Korea with Nancy Quinn.

The tour was great fun, though I can't remember what I said or did. Then, just as I was beginning to walk a straight line again without weaving, the phone rang. And I could hear a strange voice that belonged to some other girl answering, "Well, hello. How are you? Oh, I've just been on a little trip to Korea for Christmas. It was very nice. Yes, I enjoyed it very much. We saw different parts of Japan this time. Yes? Tea? Well, if you like. I'm living in a new place now. Yes, you may come over for tea tomorrow. Uh-huh, that would be fine. About two o'clock, I guess."

I looked around my empty apartment as I hung up the phone. There was a new rug on the floor, but I'd asked the landlord to take out the old Victorian furniture and put it in the basement, and he had. There were just eight shoji pillows and a giant ceramic hibachi from Hokkaido in the room, with one tiny desk where I sat, a remnant of Beverly Hills baroque. But, oh, the kitchen floor —the white vinyl tile was new. I'd just put that in. And my little Japanese teapot would work. Yes, we'd have a proper tea.

The next day I dressed carefully and prepared the tea things. A little plate of cookies, and the kettle on the stove. Bing arrived, looking marvelous. He was very gay and told me all about a trip he'd made through the South with Phil Harris. The places they'd been—the things they'd done. Such funny stories.

I served tea. It was wonderful to see him. Maybe I wouldn't have to . . . then he said, "Would you like to go to dinner Saturday night?"

"No, thank you."

"What?" He looked a little surprised.

"No, Bing. I won't go out with you anymore. I'm sorry." And I smiled. At least I tried to smile.

He looked so puzzled. He couldn't really understand. "Oh, I see." He didn't at all. He finished his tea and said, "Well, I guess I'd better be going."

"Thank you for coming by." We shook hands at the door, and he was gone. I didn't feel anything. Not happy, not sad. Only a void. But the thing was, I was living and the sun went down that evening and the sun rose the very next day, right on schedule.

I went to work. I went to work very hard—doing scenes from Shakespeare with Gloria Krieger for Benno Schneider. Oh, the things I tore through in those days. Portia, Rosalind, Hero, and Beatrice, all the younger girls in Shakespeare.

I had one bad relapse. Oh, that ghastly day. How could he do such a thing? To go to my mailbox and find a letter, delivered by hand, saying, "I shouldn't have seen you last Sunday. The visit only revived old hopes and dreams which I thought were safely interred. It'll take me another couple of months to file them away again. I called you a second time, not because I wanted to show you some pictures, but to find out how best to get these papers to you." And there was my baptismal certificate. The papers we had worked so hard to acquire in Hayden Lake—papers that were worthless now. Why did he return them? He must know how that would hurt.

From January to July—nothing.

But then came another letter. It couldn't have arrived at a more awkward time. Lillian Barkley and I were trying to get me organized to begin my nursing courses. And Mr. Cohn called with the news that I was going to be a princess in a technicolor fantasy called *The Seventh Voyage of Sinbad,* shot in Spain. *¡Qué maravilla!*

I felt much better organized than usual one morning when I made a trip to the mail room, just to see if there might be a fan letter. And there was one—an envelope with the familiar hand-writing, mailed on July 24 from Pebble Beach. It said: "Dear Kathryn. There's a nuisance lawsuit coming up for a decision soon. Nothing that concerns you or our relationship. I'm the defendant. A Mr. Dahlgren, who is handling the thing for me, may want to query you on some facts, dates, etc., to establish where I was at certain times last summer. There's absolutely no chance you will be involved in any way whatsoever, but even so I can easily appreciate why you would want to duck it. But I told him I would try. Would you be kind enough to drop me a note, 9028 Sunset Boulevard, appraising me of your reaction to this proposal. Should it be negative, I will call him off. If agreeable, he'll call you for an appointment. What is your number? Yours, Bing."

I felt quite peculiar when I'd read that letter. Although I knew I wasn't going to see Bing anymore, I was outraged that anyone would want to sue him. He had done so many things for so many people. How could anyone take advantage of him? My hands shook when I dialed his office.

"May I speak to Mr. Dahlgren, please? No, he works for Mr. Crosby. It's about a lawsuit. You don't know him? Well, I just received a message that I was to call a Mr. Dahlgren regarding a lawsuit. No, I was supposed to drop Mr. Crosby a note, but I'm leaving for Spain in two days, so if Mr. Dahlgren wants to take a deposition or anything, he can call me at this number. I'd like to know what questions he wants answered and so forth."

Would I like to call Mr. Crosby?

"No, I would not like to call Mr. Crosby, but I will be here for the next hour if he wants to call me."

I felt very grand as I hung up, then after a moment I felt frustrated. What if he didn't call? I'd just be sitting on the end of that phone forever. I'd never move—not to eat or sleep, or bathe or anything. They'd find me here, a skeleton. A very patient skeleton waiting with the phone in one hand, ready to pick it up.

Such gloomy musings were dispelled after perhaps two minutes by the phone ringing. "Hello," I gasped. "Oh, yes, this is Kathryn." I didn't have to ask who it was. "I tried to reach Mr. Dahlgren. They don't seem to know him at your office, and I'm going to Spain

in two days to make a picture called *The Seventh Voyage of Sinbad*. If you want me to talk to Mr. Dahlgren tonight or in the
morning, he can call me, or I can . . ." He didn't say anything.

Finally, after a pause, he said dryly, "And how are you?"

"I'm just fine."

"That's nice."

"Oh, well, I thought it was an emergency, or I'd never have
. . . you'll wait until I come back? Very well. Thank you. Yes,
I'm sure I'll have a good time in Spain."

And it was a whirl for me—Granada, shooting in the Alhambra
with technicolor lights illuminating those glorious Moorish ceilings, and I in a silken bed, a princess out of the Arabian nights.
And gypsies singing and dancing on the hills across the way. We
could hear them all night until dawn, which came up green with a
huge full moon slowly settling on the horizon. Then the braying of
the donkeys and the church bells began, blending in a musical
cacophony. The sounds of Spain!

Then there was the food—the ham, and white wine for breakfast, of all things. And meeting Carmencita Sanchez, the wonderful *peluquera* who cared for my hair and my makeup, and, best
of all, taught me Castillian Spanish.

And Madrid with the studios and the people and the bullfighters
who wrote me such touching letters . . . Majorca with the Cuevas
del Artá . . . Costa Brava. . . . Ah, but it was on the Costa Brava
that I really knew I wasn't cured. I'd been thinking that now I was
a big movie star. Better than Miss Fat Stock. Almost as good as
being in love, isn't it? Then on a neighboring balcony somebody
played a record called "True Love." How many hundreds of times
had I heard that record? Mostly at Hayden Lake, where we kept it
on the top of the stack, and it just played over and over. Of course
we paraphrased the middle section, "For you and I have a guardian
angel on high with *plenty* to do."

Then the letters began again. The first one I found when we
returned from Spain. I yearned to tear it open at the mailbox, but
Aunt Mary was there. So I put it on the desk with the rest of the
mail and waited until I was alone. Then, with the celerity of a sprint
champion, I raced wildly from the front door around a corner and

to the small desk, where I opened the envelope as quickly as I could without tearing everything to pieces.

The lawyer, Mr. Dahlgren, had effected a satisfactory settlement of the matter in dispute, and Mr. Dahlgren felt it would not be necessary to take my deposition. But, Bing added, he would like to see me, and he was coming to Los Angeles from Carmel in just a few days, so would I drop him a line at Mapleton, his Los Angeles home, telling him he could call?

He needed me no longer, so that was that. But I'd have to answer him. I couldn't ignore it. Though I'd advise any girl in my shoes to ignore it absolutely. But I knew myself. I couldn't ignore Bing's letter.

So I sat down and tried to express something. I decided being honest was the best policy. "Dear Bing. Yes, I still love you. No, I won't see you. Kathryn." That just about covered it.

On October 8 another note came, special delivery. I didn't answer it.

October 15: another. I held them all and ticked them off in my hand, loving them, feeling they'd be all I had to remember him by some day. The last note said he wanted to see me for a brief chat.

That Sunday the studio had sent me to appear at a hairdressers' convention. Helen Hunt had done a beautiful chignon for me with very fancy twists, and my makeup was all straight, thanks to Irving Pringle. Muriel Davidson from Publicity and I drove downtown, and I suppose she wondered why I was so quiet. I don't remember that I was thinking anything at all.

She said, while we were waiting to go on, "How would you like to see the big Edsel show? It's in here, too."

We decided to go, and when I walked in, Bing waltzed back into my life. Now I knew what it was like to be a fan.

He looked quite wonderful. Healthy, tanned, eyes sparkling. Muriel said, "What's the matter with your mascara, Kathryn? Is it getting in your eye?"

I turned away quickly. "Yes, I think I'd better go get it fixed before . . ." And I ran from the room.

Dear Army Archard, he turned cupid. I suspect Muriel told

him, but anyway Army wrote in his column, "Watching the Edsel Spec last Sunday, Kathy Grant's beautiful eyes filled with tears when Bing bounced in."

Bing's reaction came on the seventeenth: "Dear Kathryn. An apocryphal item, I'm sure. But eager to believe it, I'm emboldened to send one more appeal to you. . . ."

I was beginning to dissolve. I needed help, and fast. Father Keiser gave it to me. He was so understanding, this tall towheaded priest with a cowlick that seemed never to stay in place.

"You see, Father, he's written me these notes. He wants to see me again. I don't think I want to. I decided I wouldn't. I mean, I certainly don't want to go out for dinner, or to the Academy Awards again. We've done that." I tried so hard to be calm, but I felt the large lump coming back in my throat. "Father, I don't know *what* to do."

"You're doing fine, Sis. Just keep out of it. Don't do a thing."

"You don't think I should write him—or, better still, fly to his arms?"

"No, I don't. Just don't do anything."

Then on Tuesday, October 22, came another note. I carried it carefully to my room, tortured myself for a while by examining the envelope before I opened it. There was no postmark. It had been delivered by hand. This time I knew I had to answer. "Marriage, any time, any place you wish," it said.

Of course I wanted marriage to the one man I could not live without. Had he felt the silence of the months past as I had? He must have.

All through the night I tossed and pondered, fear sweeping over me in waves, only to be supplanted by a tingling sort of joy. Toward dawn I knew the answer, the only answer possible. The only answer I could ever have given him, from the first "Hi, Tex" on the Paramount lot.

But I was not a child now as I had been then. No, certain promises had been made, broken, made again. I would proceed maturely with caution. The first thing I would do was call Aunt Mary, have breakfast and then, around ten o'clock, proceed to plan my future.

When I phoned Aunt Mary, she was talking to Bing on her other line. And she, of all people, was crying. "He sounds so lonely," she said. "He sounds so sad. He wants to talk to you and I can't give him your number because you know I promised I wouldn't."

"I'll be right over," I gasped. But I found I couldn't talk to him myself. Not then. I was trembling too much. My maturity had gone down the drain with the toothpaste.

Half an hour later Aunt Mary and Bing were once more on the phone, while I sat nearby hugging a cup of tea and wondering idly what fate had in store for me. Plans were discussed: transportation, assembly points, evasive action because of reporters. I ventured only one query. Could I continue my nursing? And acting, could I continue that? Not that I was any Duse, but Columbia was beginning to have faith in me.

I went to the studio for my work with Benno Schneider. For some reason my concentration was minimal that day. At three I called Aunt Mary, who was frantic and jubilant, an incongruous combination.

"We're taking the five o'clock plane, young lady," she told me.

The bubble bath that evening in Las Vegas was warm and, since I would not be there long, I used almost a whole bottle. There was enough billowy foam to fill the tub and overflow onto the floor. I flipped some of it off my nose, trying to appear nonchalant while Aunt Mary was on the telephone. I knew it must be Bing.

When she hung up I queried, "Well, what did he say?"

She came prancing into the bathroom and sat on the lid of the "convenience" to give me a detailed play-by-play description. "Well, the funniest thing happened, Kathryn. He called about an hour ago from the Sands Hotel and the man down at the desk said, 'I'm sorry, we don't have anyone at the Desert Inn registered as Mrs. Guilbert Banks. No, there's no Olive Banks either.'" (Olive was me, because of the press.) "He just reached me and was frantic. He thought we might have gotten cold feet and fled Las Vegas. I told him that we don't do that sort of thing. We keep our end of the bargain. Of course there was nothing he could say then. He wanted to come right on over, but I told him that you were bathing and were tired, and that tomorrow would be a very big day. So perhaps we'd better just meet in the morning at seven-thirty. He agreed. Leo's going to pick us up, and all the arrangements seem to be made.

"Now, you'd better get out of that tub and into bed or you won't be a very radiant bride tomorrow."

I lay there incredulous. Well, he hadn't disappeared yet. Anyway, I'd better get some sleep.

"The important thing, Kathryn," said Aunt Mary as I emerged from the tub, "he seems to love you very much." Her brown eyes started to fill with tears. "If I didn't think so, I certainly never would have come up here with you." And here her square jaw line set in determined thought.

"Well, Aunt Mary, I hope your trip works out better than mine. I've been on the road for three years now and a fat lot of good it's done me. Here I am, still a bachelor girl—and getting kind of used to it now. It's really not a bad life."

I dropped my towel and slid into shorty PJ's, shuddering inwardly. If the wedding did go through, would I have the nerve to put on that filmy robe with its lace peignoir? It even had a *train,* deliver me!

The plush carpet scrunched between my toes and softened the ultraslick, ultramodern, ultra-ultra look of the room. I flicked back the spread and Aunt Mary admonished, "If I were you I'd fold that spread neatly and tomorrow night try to impress Bing with your tidiness."

"Aunt Mary, do you want me to start off marriage with a lie?"

"Well, you don't have to disillusion him all at once."

What an idea—fold the bedspread! And me with a pleated chiffon train. I dived under the covers.

"Listen! We've paid the rent for next month, haven't we? I mean just in case. . . ."

"Oh, go to sleep, Katie, and stop being sassy."

Sassy? Why shouldn't I be sassy? I was only getting married again—maybe. On the fifth, or was it the sixth attempt. I suddenly felt teary. "Goodnight, Aunt Mary. Thank you for being with me.

And thank you and Uncle Guil for being my friends for all these years."

"Goodnight, Katie, I just hope Bing will appreciate you and love you, and that you'll have a good life together."

"Ummmmm." I lay there, eyes closed, pretending to be asleep. No need to alarm Aunt Mary. *She'd* never planned to marry Bing before.

My wedding day dawned. I had all Bing's little notes and the letter from Monsignor Kincannon, and my birth and baptismal certificates. When it was time to get up, I held them close to me for a minute. Would my guardian angel get me through it this time?

Aunt Mary was awake, ordering coffee. I started to dress, thinking of all the other days, all the other places where I'd planned to don wedding clothes: Carmel, Hayden Lake, Texas, and now here I was dressing at the Desert Inn in Las Vegas. It wouldn't be the navy-blue Jean-Louis suit, or the white brocade gown. Just a simple white suit and a hat.

My lipstick went on straight, and the circles under my eyes were hidden by careful makeup. I *was* tired, but the sparkle couldn't be hidden by anything. Somewhere, deep down, I was beginning to hear a voice that said, *This time it really might come true—it really might.*

I slid into my suit and borrowed Aunt Mary's stole, putting on some dark glasses. "Kathryn, if you want not to call attention to yourself, I wouldn't wear those glasses until you get into the lobby. You look like you're about to hold up a bank, dear." My laugh cracked somewhere in the middle.

I wanted to call Mother, but I didn't dare—someone might overhear the call.

"Now, Kathryn, remember what you said last night? Getting married is quite a simple thing. Lots of people do it."

I looked at Aunt Mary for a long thirty seconds. I felt sheer terror overwhelm me. "Oh, Aunt Mary, it isn't! It's awful. I don't want to get married. I don't want to marry Bing even if I do love him. I'd like to go home."

"Hush. We're due in the lobby right now."

We walked down the hall and a wave of nausea swept over me. "Aunt Mary, I don't feel at all well."

"You're just hungry. Come on. Your church is absolutely pagan not to let people eat before receiving Communion."

"No, Aunt Mary, there's something about the sacrament . . ."

"Let's not talk theology today, young lady; just march."

We reached the lobby and Leo Lynn met us. He was the only person there. He boomed, "Happy is the bride when the sun shines." My stomach knotted up tight, and I wanted to throw up.

Aunt Mary admonished, "Hush, Leo. This thing is supposed to be a secret, and anyway the saying is 'Happy is the bride that the sun shines on.'"

I said nothing. Was the sun shining? Perhaps it wasn't. I certainly didn't feel very happy.

We got into the car and drove to the parking lot at the Sands Hotel. There was Bing. He was dressed in a navy blue pinstripe suit, wearing a Tyrolean hat, and looking astonishingly handsome. He said, "Good morning," very jovially.

They all looked at me, expecting me to respond, but I just couldn't, so I nodded. Aunt Mary started to get out of the car so Bing could sit by me, but she didn't get far. I had her arm. Bing sat in front with Leo, and we drove to the courthouse.

Leo came to a stop, and Bing opened the door. We started up the steps, and he took my arm. His touch didn't steady me at all. It made me dizzy. It made me want to kiss him and tell him how I had missed him during the whole year past. I wanted to cry. I wanted to scream. The steps kept moving backward beneath my feet—twenty-seven, twenty-eight, twenty-nine—and then we were inside the dark, quiet building. The license bureau was nearly empty as we began to fill out forms. Olive Kathryn Grandstaff. Born—Houston, Texas. Harry Lillis Crosby. Born—Tacoma, Washington.

A reporter walked in casually on his daily beat, did a big take, and advanced on us. By then I knew the score. This was it. I liked the press. Reporters as well as reviewers had been kind to me, particularly in the last year. Because of their kindness, I had a good role in a new Western, *Gunman's Walk,* with Van Heflin. Wardrobe fittings were to be that afternoon. Now, if I took a ten o'clock plane, I could make the fittings and deny ever having been in Nevada. This flashed through my no-longer-addled brain. I started for the front door before the reporter's query was over.

"Bing, are you getting married?" I heard dimly.

Bing executed a graceful half-pirouette, caught me by the elbow, and his voice evinced pleasure at the reporter's interest. "Why —yes, yes, as a matter of fact, we are. Kathryn and I are driving over to Yarington near Reno. Father Lahive is going to marry us about five this afternoon. Love to have you join us." The surprised reporter dropped his notebook and flew out the door.

"Now, Miss Grandstaff, next stop is St. Anne's, right around the corner." Bing ushered me out masterfully. Actually St. Anne's was about a mile from the courthouse, and Leo stopped at the rectory.

The Right Reverend John J. Ryan greeted us in whispers and quickly took us into his study, where we filled out more papers. Then he took us to the church and bolted the doors. Suddenly I remembered an anguished letter I had written to my mother back in Texas: "Mother, I'll never see him again unless it's in church with the doors bolted."

"It's highly unusual to do a thing like this," he said, "but we don't want people bothering us. And besides, I don't have my own vestments. I was going to Ireland two days ago and missed my flight, though my luggage made it. And then, Bing, when you called up, I decided I'd better miss another flight and help you out." How could he treat this all so lightly? Perhaps two years ago I could have been gay. Perhaps a year ago I could still have been casual about it. Now I was overwhelmed with the awful responsibility of marriage—anyone's marriage. I was terribly afraid. I was numb.

The nuptial Mass that I had studied in Spokane two years before with Father Corkery was engraved on my brain, and as Monsignor Ryan spoke the ritual, Father Corkery's voice echoed curiously in my ears.

We were all alone in the church, Bing and I, Mary Banks and Leo, Father Ryan, and two startled altar boys. Bing led me up to the altar inside the rail, where we pledged our troth. His voice was firm and clear, mine sounded very far away and not quite of this world.

Finally: *Ite missa est. Deo gratias.* And we went back into the little room where Monsignor Ryan removed his borrowed vestments. Finally it dawned on me that Bing and I were married. Mr. and Mrs. Harry Lillis Crosby were thanking the priest.

We looked at each other. I think neither of us really believed what had happened, but there were Leo and Aunt Mary, beaming, and on the fourth finger of my left hand was a thin gold band.

Bing moved closer to me, and instead of a kiss, gave me a light pat on the cheek. "Well, Mrs. Crosby, shall we inform the press it's a *fait accompli?* It's pretty hot for them to drive all the way to Yarington today."

There was a small wedding breakfast at Bing's hotel, with toasts and things. I talked with my family, and he with his. As we drove to the airport to catch the plane to Palm Springs, Bing asked in all sincerity, "Mary, why don't you come to Palm Desert with us?"

"Now, Bing, I've gotten you two this far. You'll manage without me pretty well. Besides, Guil expects me home at noon."

Once on the plane I found the power of speech had returned at last. "You know, Bing, last night I was thinking about our—our courtship. I think I owe a debt of gratitude to Mr. Dahlgren. If it hadn't been for that lawsuit, I never could have talked with you again, and you would have been spared this fatal step."

"What do you mean, 'spared'? I created Dahlgren."

"Created . . . ?"

"Made him up! Invented him."

"You . . . but why?"

"Because"—and he looked at me intensely for a few seconds, and I thought he was going to say something profound. "Because, my little Texas tomato, I couldn't bear to live without you."

We were halfway to Palm Springs before I stopped crying.

CHAPTER 3

How To Live with a Mother-in-law

I reached for a pair of slacks. It was chilly in the spring morning, and with good reason—it was only six thirty. But then I drew back my hand. This was the day I should look a bit more proper. I eyed the man's suit rack, which served as a closet in the dressing room that had once been a nursery. Yes, that would do it—the Jean-Louis walking suit with a full skirt featuring little patches. There were short sleeves I could work in and a jacket which would cover my arms. I knew Mother Crosby didn't like bare backs or fronts, but I wasn't certain about bare arms. Better be on the safe side this morning.

I wasn't sure this was going to work anyway. It was a very long shot. But what were the alternatives? Pretty grim. If I failed, there was nothing to do but pack and leave, and all over a "nice warm tub bath," for heaven's sake.

Of course if I did leave, it would be just the reverse of my entry to Mapleton, when *her* bags were packed. Bing and I had come home after our four-day honeymoon. He had to work, and I had to work, and we couldn't stay away any longer. There she was, the chauffeur waiting at the door.

"Congratulations, and I'm leaving."

We had only just arrived and here we were, coaxing her to stay.

"No reflection on Kathryn, of course," she said. "It's just that no roof is big enough for two families. I had a wonderful life with my husband, and I only came here because Bing needed me to help with his boys. Now they're grown up, and you two are married, and you have a right to have your own home to yourselves."

Catherine Harrigan Crosby meant it. She wasn't angling for us to coax her to stay. She was completely sincere, but Bing and I instinctively decided we'd have none of this, naturally. We induced her to stay by telling her we needed her. Still, she always made us feel that this was our home and she was just a guest.

But then came the hot-bath affair. Even Olive Kathryn Grandstaff never pulled a more glaring boner.

So on this frigid morning I quietly stomped my way downstairs. The hall seemed very long to the butler's pantry. Once the lights were on and the big restaurant-type range was heating the kettle for tea, I felt warmer and thought a little more clearly.

How grateful I was that we had convinced Mrs. Crosby of our need for her. I hadn't been in 594 South Mapleton Drive for twenty minutes before I realized how true it was.

It was she who faced with me all the problems of early marriage and gave me so much good advice. Real help, not just mother-in-law platitudes. For instance, on our first night there, when I walked into Bing's room, there was the double bed, and on that double bed was a blanket cover, beautifully monogrammed: *DLC*. Then, when I went to dress that night in Bing's bath, the first thing my eye saw was a big picture of a gorgeous blonde, a beauty with a soft tender face, smiling gently. It was inscribed "To my angel, Bing." That must have been their special term of endearment to each other because all Bing had ever told me about Dixie was that she was an angel; that she'd been a wonderful mother to their four sons. He told me no more than that, but I felt he had loved her devotedly, deeply, and that their years of marriage had meant the world to him.

I had never seen her, never met her. She had died several years before I met Bing. Yet, when I saw her portrait and the monogram on the blanket cover, I was jealous, and thought, What am I doing here?

I thought I might mention it to Bing, and at breakfast I opened my mouth like a guppy once or twice, but I just didn't know what to say. I wanted to call my mother. I even picked up the phone and dialed half the number, but I was sure Mother would say, "You're married now, dear. You must work out your own problems."

Bing hadn't even noticed. And I'm sure I wouldn't have been so conscious of it all if it hadn't been for that incident at Palm Desert.

Next morning I lingered over coffee with Bing's mother. "Mrs. Crosby, I wonder if I could have a talk with you?"

"Of course, Kathryn. Shall we go to the library?"

She led me down the long hall, past the Munnings hunting scene with the red-coated gentlemen riding to hounds, past the two beautiful portraits of the boys—Gary and Lindsay in one picture, and Dennis and Phillip in another—and into the paneled library with its flowered curtains and curved window seat. "Now sit down, Kathryn. What would you like to talk to me about?"

"Well, I haven't been married very long, but I know you had a long and happy marriage, and you must be good at solving problems, and . . . well . . . I wake up every morning and see the picture of the first Mrs. Crosby, and I have her blanket cover on my bed, and I don't know—I mean, it feels so strange. What . . . can't I do something? What do you think I should do?"

Mrs. Crosby looked at me with great understanding and smiled and said, "Well, dear, I don't think I'd do anything. Why don't you just get dressed and go to work this morning, and I'm sure everything will be just fine." She dismissed me and my problem.

So there was nothing to do. I'd just have to live with it. So, that was that! But Bing's mother seemed very warm and very nice. I had a feeling right then that we'd get along because she didn't laugh at me; yet she didn't make a fuss over me.

I got dressed and went to the studio, and when I came home that evening, I discovered that the picture wasn't there any longer. And the blanket cover on the bed was a plain one—a pure-white blanket cover. The Madonna that Mrs. Crosby had given us for our wedding was on my bedside stand.

I went flying through the house to find her, gave her a big hug, and danced her around in a circle. "Oh, thank you, Mother, thank you." She blushed absolutely scarlet. The Irish, it seems, aren't always very demonstrative.

"Ahem." She coughed a little bit. "Tell me, how was Palm Desert? Do you like Bing's new house down there? I used to like Palm Desert a lot. Very pretty view of the valley."

"Oh, Mrs. Crosby, I think you'd love the new house. Of course I love it because he built it the year we didn't see each other, and it's precious to me because I think it was his way of trying to forget me. You drive up and there's a della Robbia, a beautiful Madonna and Child, set right into the red adobe walls. And there's the Crosby crest set into the tile of the entrance floor. And there's a big Spanish door. Bing said it came from the Hearst place. But he carried me over the threshold."

"Did he really? That's nice," Mrs. Crosby said perfunctorily.

Now it was my time to blush. I felt I was gushing a little. "Well, yes. And the dining room is not really a dining room. That and the living room are all one except there's a wall and iron grill between, and the living room's down a couple of steps."

"I don't like steps too much."

"But there's a rail. I'm sure you'd do all right. And the dining room table is an Elizabethan melon-ball table."

"A what?"

"A melon-ball table. The legs are in the shape of big melons— sort of one sitting on top of another . . . except Bing did the most terrible thing."

"What did he do?"

"He cut one of the melon balls off each leg of the table because they said the table was too high."

"What a peculiar thing to do. Why couldn't he get higher chairs?"

"He said they didn't think it would be right because the desert house has very low ceilings, like all the houses there, and I guess that Elizabethan table was built for houses with ceilings twenty feet high. It still has a ledge that you put your feet on to keep them off the cold floor.

"And in the living room there are some very nice sofas, built in.

They're very hard, so you don't sink down into them, and that's probably good for the desert, don't you think? Cooler, and you don't get sticky. And Bing had a coffee table made out of a piece of carrara glass that he'd found in a candy factory in Carmel."

"Oh, I know that place. My bridge partner, Laura Hendricks, and I used to go there to get chocolates years ago."

"Bing showed me the house and said, 'Well, dear, how do you like what I've been doing this year while you've not been speaking to me?' I was of course overwhelmed and said, 'For me?' Just then Pete Petitto, who had driven us in from the airport and who works for Bing—"

"Oh yes, I know Pete. He was in the service with all those radio writers, and he's worked for Bing for quite a while now."

"Yes, that's the one. Well, he yelled from the bedroom, 'Hey, Bing, we'll have to get another bed in here. The single's not enough!' "

Mrs. Crosby seemed only somewhat amused. She said, "What's the kitchen like?" This got us on to a subject more suitable for development.

"It has a built-in breakfast booth."

"A what?"

"A table and a booth that's built in. You sort of slide the table out. It's very pretty. And there's a gas range, built in. It should work very well, although I didn't have very good luck with it at first. And there's an icebox with built-in ice maker."

"Well, that's a lot handier than when we had to buy ice in blocks and bring it down from the icehouse in a wagon drawn by a horse."

"Funny, that's the only industry they had in West Columbia when I left—an ice plant. But you know, Mrs. Crosby, Bing told me that he himself, with Howard Lapham, designed the house. They walked along the ground and just drew the plans out with a stick in the sand."

"That's only natural, Kathryn. You know, my father—Bing's grandfather—was a contractor."

"He was?"

"Oh, yes. He built many fine buildings in the Tacoma-Seattle area. Churches, schools, big buildings. And besides that, Bing has built seven houses, you have to remember. He built one down at Rancho Santa Fe, did some reconstruction work there, and then with the aid of his father-in-law, Mr. Wyatt, he built the house over in the valley."

"You mean the one that burned down that Christmas?"

"Yes. That was the one. And then Hayden Lake."

I winced. Yes, there was always Hayden Lake.

"I think that's a very pretty house. Do you?"

"Yes—it's very pretty." All I could remember of Hayden Lake was that ghastly boat house and the recalcitrant boat, and how miserable I'd been.

"There's a very nice pool. The house is sort of a Y shape, and the inside of the Y faces out on the pool and overlooks the valley below, and the purple mountains. In the spring they're all purple with verbena or yellow with marguerites. But Bing's color-blind and can't tell one from another."

"Oh, but it's just on reds that he's color-blind, isn't it, Mrs. Crosby? He can tell blues and greens and things like that."

"No, greens and browns baffle him. Another inherited trait. His father had great trouble with pinks and greens."

"Oh, tell me about him."

"Well, he was just wonderful. I liked him the minute I met him. I met Harry in church. Took us a long time to get married, but he was a very happy person, loved music, very happy-go-lucky and jolly. Everybody loved him. Times were pretty hard once in a while, but still we managed to get all seven children through high school and as much college as they wanted. That's saying something."

"Did they all go to Gonzaga?"

"The boys did. Bing was going into law until he decided to come to Hollywood, but he'd finished his four years. You finished college?"

"Yes, ma'am. University of Texas—1955, Bachelor of Fine Arts." When Mrs. Crosby asked a question, you answered clearly and quickly.

"You smoke?"

"No, ma'am, I never have."

"You drink?"

"Well, a little wine now and then."

She nodded. "And the boys? You've met them?"

"Oh, yes, Mrs. Crosby. Lindsay came down the day after we were married. He and his girl friend, Sally, came down to go swimming."

"Lindsay's too young to get serious about anyone."

"Well, we were glad to see them and I think they had a good time. It was pretty exciting down there with all the flowers and wires coming in. Of course I did the most terrible thing."

"What was that?"

"Well, I wasn't really prepared for a wedding trip, I didn't even know where we'd go for a honeymoon or anything. I really hadn't even talked to Bing until the day we were married; and I had only a couple of wool dresses and a pair of shorts and a bathing suit. So, after I'd been swimming I put on the tennis shorts to sit around the pool with Lindsay and Sally, and Bing came out and rather sternly said, 'I think those shorts are just fine for writing letters in your room. They look more like Sunset Strip than Abercrombie and Fitch.' So I went in and put on a wool dress and sweltered."

Mother smiled and nodded complete approval of Bing's decision.

"Oh, there was one thing that happened that I'd love for you to know about."

"What was that?"

"My first party meal. Alice and Phil Harris had fed us quail, and macaroni and cheese on our first evening, and Alice sent up chickens to broil, and casseroles that could be easily warmed over. She'd been such a help, so I thought the Sunday before we left Palm Desert we'd ask them up for supper.

"Bing agreed, and I planned a dinner of lamb chops because they say anybody can cook lamb chops, some string beans, rice and gravy, and a green salad. There was also going to be a really special fruit mold for dessert. In a red jellied base I put all kinds of pears, peaches, marshmallows, Bing cherries, slices of apple, all arranged exquisitely. It took hours. I slid it all into the refrigerator first, knowing that at least one course was going to be beautiful.

"There was still some wedding cake left, which would help. I set the table at two in the afternoon to be well organized, and Bing went to play golf so I could worry these things out by myself, which was a blessing.

"He got back about five saying that Alice and Phil were sorry, but Alice had a cold and couldn't come to dinner. I must admit I was relieved. By that time things were desperate. I had tried to whip cream for the dessert, using a dry milk powder in the blender with a little lemon juice for flavoring. After the ice water reconstituted the crystals, the lemon juice curdled it instead of flavoring it—and then, as I kept whipping it, it got hotter and hotter and turned sour. That went down the sink first.

"Next I put the lamb chops in the oven. They looked beautiful. They had on paper panties (or rather, toreador pants). I don't know what I was thinking—perhaps that they were asbestos. Of course the whole thing caught fire. Smoke poured out. By the time I had used Bing's new dish towels to beat out the flames, the chops were charred."

Mrs. Crosby chuckled. "I think I'm going to have to give you a few lessons in the kitchen."

"Oh, but that's not the worst part, Mother. The gravy looked like wallpaper paste and tasted that way, the rice had boiled over, and the bottom layer was cemented to the pot. The rest looked like parched Indian corn. I wished we'd brought a cook on our honeymoon."

"I should think so."

"Bing was pretty hungry by then, so I took the fruit mold in for him to see. He was impressed. It was really beautiful. I suppose he consoled himself with the thought that we were going back to our courtship days when he had eaten birthday cake and we'd had no dinner at all. So I went into the kitchen and held the beautiful mold under the hot water to loosen it. I loosened it all right —*slurp!* There was a horrific gurgling sound as the entire thing glided slowly down the garbage disposal like a large ruby-red jellyfish.

"Bing called from the next room, 'Kathryn, are you all right? That sounded like a sound effect from an Alec Guinness movie.' 'It was just your dinner, dear.' He took one look, got my coat, and said, 'I can dine out for weeks on this story. Let's go down the hill for a hamburger.' "

"That wasn't the smoothest beginning to a marriage, but it's like Bing to laugh about it. He has always been kind to me—besides, he doesn't upset easily."

"He was pretty upset Sunday, and so was I."

"What happened, dear?"

"Well, after the Saturday-night dinner fiasco and Bing's joking reaction, I was confident that life would be a lark. But we went to Mass, and as we entered the church, the old Robert Louis Stevenson lines rang through my head, 'The world is so full of a number of things, I'm sure we should all be as happy as kings.' I should have recalled Dorothy Parker's realistic addition, 'And you know how happy kings are.'

"There were a few smiles from parishioners as we walked down the aisle, but one woman fixed me with an icy glare. That's curious, I thought. What's wrong with her? Maybe she looks at everyone like that.

"Then we took our pace in an empty pew. When Mass was over, we knelt and then started to leave the church when suddenly this woman burst through the crowd screaming and shouting hysterically at Bing and me.

" 'How dare you marry this tramp?' she shrieked. 'And you, you bitch, what do you mean taking the man I love away from me?' Her face was contorted with fury and her eyes were blazing. Poor soul, she must have been crazy. Several people tried to restrain her, but she broke loose and I thought she was going to hit me. She raised her arm, then screamed at Bing, 'How could you do this to Dixie? How could you do this to your boys who need you? How could you do this to *me?*'

"Bing suddenly became active and protective. He stepped between us, his eyes steely, faced her, and growled, 'How can you behave like this in the house of the Lord? Shut up and get out.'

"She slunk away like a whipped puppy, and the rest of us silently left church. I was trembling. Not so much with fright as in awe at the change in Bing, habitually so easygoing. He was in a barely controlled fury. I never knew he could be so violent."

"Good heavens, what an experience!" Mother gasped. "Who was she?"

"Bing told me she was an addled fan who has been haunting him off and on for several years, writing crackpot letters full of wild protestations; but this outburst was too much. 'Next time we'll have to drop the net on her,' he said. Actually, I think he felt sorry for her."

"Kathryn, you must know that we all have fierce tempers. We don't anger easily, but we don't forgive easily either."

I went to the front door for the morning paper. The cool dawn air brushed away the cobwebs and I leaned on the iron grill studying the jacaranda and pepper trees and the big star inlaid in the forecourt. Then back around to the rose garden, that oval area patterned after a Sheraton design, with pillars all around and rambler roses draped over the chains that linked the pillars. I started gathering roses, intending to get only one bud for Mother's tray. But then I couldn't stop.

I looked out over the lawn and thought of all the Sundays I had spent at the Crosbys' before and since marriage, when Mrs. Crosby, in baseball cap and sunglasses, would be hostess for all four boys and their budding families. On these days it looked like an incipient kindergarten or a summer camp. Each wife would bring her specialty: French bread, salad, ham, hors d'oeuvres. I always contributed something substantial from the kitchen, like macaroni. There had to be some solid items for those hearty appetites.

The little ones would swing on the swings or ride on the seesaws. And we'd picnic on the lawn and watch the wild games of touch football. And the dialogue in Crosbyese flew. After a violent touch that was closer to a tackle, "Stay on your feet, Lin, you may get a draw." Or, if one of us girls wore slacks that were on the form-fitting side, one of the boys would remark, "Looks like a sack of cats on the way to the river." Once Gary complimented his Dad on what a good housewife I'd become. Bing responded, "Oh, she's okay, I guess, but she cuts easy." Deep research later disclosed to me that it was a boxing term, indicating a fighter too sensitive for his profession.

When we were all on the lawn with the children and really gossiping away, which interfered with the radio reception of some big ball game, Phil would shout, "Cool it, you gals, sounds like daybreak on a guinea farm."

My favorite Crosbyism was an overheard remark, not meant for my ears, when Bing was describing a recent duck hunt that we'd been on at the ranch. We'd risen at five in the morning and I'd sleepily prepared ham and eggs and toast, and donned all those sets of long underwear needed before we went out on the levee. The sun had risen in a burst of glory, and so had the ducks—all going straight up at sixty miles an hour.

Bing had been a little disgruntled that day and though we threw plenty of lead in the air, our score was closer to zero than limit, but as he told it to the boys, he philosophized grimly, "I couldn't hit a bull in the ass with a plate of spinach."

The stories Mrs. Crosby told at these times were every bit up to the standards set by the other Crosbys. When the girls were complaining, quite naturally, about the boys' nightclub act, and how they had to be on the road so many weeks a month, she said, "You know, when Bing's dad used to go to the ball games, I was home with seven children, and I'd wait until he came in. But when he got there, I'd meet him at the door with my hat on. Supper for everybody was on the stove, and I knew he could dish it out. I would never say anything at all, or offer any explanation; I'd just go. I'd come back when I felt good and ready."

"But Mother," I gasped, "where could you go in a town like Spokane?"

"Oh, I went up to the Sholderers—Wilma, Bertha, Mary, Margaret, and Rose. I could always have a cup of tea and a visit there and stay as long as I wanted. But Harry never knew where I was. Sometimes," she added with her blue eyes twinkling, "I came back as late as midnight."

"I had a friend," she continued merrily, "whose husband was 'fond of a drop.' In fact, he'd occasionally come home intoxicated. Well, my friend managed to cure him of lingering at the tavern too long. Once about two in the morning she could hear him coming down the block singing, so she lighted one of his strong, strong cigars, blew several puffs around the room before putting it, still lit, in the ash tray. Then she set the rocker to rocking, and quickly ran to the bedroom and climbed into bed. He walked in, surveyed the scene, and didn't leave the house for months after that."

No, she understood the problems of young marriages very well. She was so thoughtful of ours. Any time Bing was home and I asked her to lunch, she'd say, "Oh, I'll just have a tray in my room for lunch. I have my big meal at night, you know." And if I asked her for dinner, she'd say, "Oh, thank you, dear, but I have my big meal at noon, you know."

An amazing bundle of contradictions, this tiny woman—only five feet two—she stood so tall, so strong. None of her girls ever smoked or drank in front of her. And I was so proud of Bing one Christmas Day when the drawing room was full of guests and she said as he was preparing his second drink, "Bing, you're drinking too much." He put the glass down and said, "I'm sorry, Mother," without a trace of embarrassment or pique.

She and Bing had the most wonderful relationship. Both were avid baseball fans and during the season their routine was practically a ritual if a game was being telecast. Right after breakfast they would repair to the drawing room, put their feet up on comfortable stools, and sit there, Mother always rooting for the Dodgers, Bing for the Pirates. Bing would remonstrate futilely, "But Mother, I'm a stockholder in the Pirates; I'm Vice President." "No matter," she'd say grimly, "I like the Dodgers. Why didn't you buy stock in them?" I have to admit she was right.

She was just as elegant in that baseball cap as when riding beautifully bonneted in the chauffeur-driven Rolls Royce going to or from the races. She always sallied forth wearing her mink and terribly excited about prospects for the day, though she never bet more than two dollars, and that on the favorite to show. As she came in the front door afterward, she would say without fail, "Back home and broke."

Her weekly bridge session with Laura Hendricks and her other friends was greatly anticipated. She always had her hair done at Helen Hunt's just before this big event, and *sometimes* she won a quarter. Today was the day for one of those meetings. I wondered if she'd go. Certainly if I didn't take her breakfast, she wouldn't.

As I put the rosebuds on the tray and got the silver and china in order, I thought, How stupid I was last night. I'd behaved almost as badly as the nurse who had taken care of Mrs. Crosby after her cataract was removed. She'd been so patronizing with her editorial "we." She bustled around saying, "Now, Mother, we're going to have our breakfast. Now, Mother, we're going to sit up in our chair. Now, Mother, we mustn't touch our eye pads."

The last straw was when she cooed, "Now, Mother, we're going to take our bath." At that Catherine Harrigan Crosby drew herself up and spoke with clarity and finality, "I am *not* your mother. My name is Mrs. Crosby, and I bathe alone."

I started making cream of wheat in the double boiler, still feeling sorry for myself. If I just hadn't taken rehabilitation nursing at the hospital, I wouldn't have come up with all those modern ideas about "improving geriatric environment." All it really meant was fixing Mrs. Crosby's room so she could be safe and comfortable. She seemed pretty safe and comfortable as she was.

But as she had mentioned cold feet and a sore back to me, I was bound and determined to get her into a warm nightly tub bath for therapy. The doctor said it was a good idea. He even gave me a special oil to put in it to help her dry skin, and told me where to get a safety bar to attach to the side of the big pink marble tub.

So, just before dinner last night, after installing the hand bar, I'd said, "Ah, Mother, how would you like to take a tub bath?" (Almost as bad as "Now, Mother, it's time for our bath," isn't it?)

She had responded just as brightly and energetically, "I bathe from the washbasin. I don't feel comfortable in that big tub. I'm not sure I can get in and out of it anymore."

"But," said I, "come look at this nice safety bar. With it you'll spring in and out like a woodland nymph."

She had laughed and said, "I don't think so, dear. Maybe another time."

That was when I should have admitted defeat. I blundered on, "But Mother, the doctor said the best thing for your cold feet and sore back would be a nice long tub bath."

"Do you mean you've been discussing my bathing with the doctor?" she had gasped.

"But Mother, he's a man of science. Those things don't matter to men of science."

"Well, they matter to me. I'm not sure I approve of that conversation at all."

"Now look, Mother, if you'd just get into the tub and sit for fifteen minutes, I'll give you a back rub and you'll rest ever so well. You won't wake up at two o'clock in the morning as you've been doing recently."

"Do I disturb you when I waken?"

"No, of course not, but I know that you're not sleeping and that worries me."

"Well, I don't want to take a bath tonight. Maybe tomorrow."

"Mrs. Crosby, as a nurse I must request that you take a bath."

"You're not a nurse yet, young lady, and don't tell me what to do."

"Now, Mother!"

"Listen here. I'm going to call Larry. If you don't like the way I do things, I'm going to move to a hotel."

"Oh, would you like me to pack your bag?" As soon as I said it, I felt a complete ass.

"Kathryn, don't you talk to me like that."

"I'm sorry, but if you'd like to go, I think it's only right that you be allowed to go. I'll help you pack your bags and I'll even call a taxi."

She drew herself up to her full five feet two, looked at me stonily for a moment, and then said quietly, "Young lady, you're tired. Go to bed this instant."

And I did!

Now, with her breakfast tray and much trepidation, I knocked on the door. And there she was, sitting up in bed, looking quite beautiful. The blue eyes that Bing had inherited were bright and shiny. Her hair was in perfect order. She was wearing a full-length pink robe, and at her throat she wore a pearl and amethyst pin. Her earrings were in place. Lipstick was on—very pale, but very straight. She looked as if she were ready to hold court.

"Good morning, Mother. I have your tray."

"Good morning, Kathryn. Isn't that very heavy for you? Come in."

I put the tray carefully on the table. "Would you like some tea?"

"Oh, no, thank you, Mother. I'll have breakfast with the children in a minute downstairs. Did you rest well?"

"Yes, thank you, dear."

It was as if nothing had happened—nothing at all.

"Kathryn, tell me about this Alan Fisher and his wife who are coming to be with us."

"Well, Mother, I met them at Cranbourne Court. At least I met Alan. Their references are fantastic. The letters are covered with crests and seals. Norma, that's Mrs. Fisher, was at Clarence House, and then Buckingham Palace. And she's worked for the Duke and Duchess of Windsor, and the Duke of Sutherland. Fisher's worked at Government House in Ottawa, and for the Duke of Buccleuch, and then for the Windsors, where he met Norma. Now they are working together for Mr. and Mrs. Solomon."

"Why in the world would they want to come and work for us?"

"Well, I'm not sure, Mother. I think they want to come to America. But more important, after talking with Mr. Fisher for a while, I think he would enjoy the kind of life we lead. They like travel. They like excitement, and certainly there's plenty of that. They seem to like small children, and when I told him you were the head of the family, he was terribly impressed."

Mother's eyes glinted delightedly. "Well, now we have a Rolls Royce and an English butler. That's pretty grand. Can we live up to them, do you think?"

"After the interview, Bing asked me how I thought they'd feel working with Miss Fat Stock."

"He did, did he?" chuckled Mother. "What did you say?"

"I retorted that I'd also been a Splash Day Princess. And we're getting a touch of the Irish to compensate for all this British grandeur. Bing thought of it. Bridget Brennan is going to join us from Ireland to help with the children. She's been working with a very sick child for three years, so our healthy ones should pose no problems. And I found out just yesterday that during her holidays, she took a course in hairdressing. Isn't that a special qualification? But of course the real reason Bing's determined she must work for us is that she comes from County Tipperary and is a left-handed golfer."

Mother nodded approvingly. The Crosbys were holding their own. "By the way, this morning I noticed in my dressing room a strange new contraption on the side of my tub. What's that?"

"It's a safety bar, Mother. If you hold on tight to that, and then the bar across, you can get in and out of the tub without danger of slipping."

"I see. Well, I think in the next day or two, I'd like a tub bath. Might make my back feel better."

CHAPTER 4

How To Have a Baby—or Three

"Please hurry, Doctor."

"You have plenty of time, Kathryn. I'll park the car and you and Dot go on up."

We sneaked in the side door of the maternity entrance, and then cut around to the left, avoiding the front desk. We all knew we could go up in the service elevator. Dr. Moss had practiced at Queen of Angels Hospital for nearly twenty years and Dotty was not only his wife, but a registered nurse—and my friend in need.

There wasn't time to take the big elevator up to the maternity wing. I must have looked like an orphan in Dotty's blue robe, much too big for me, and her daughter's blue slippers. I shrank from the curious eyes in the waiting room and the registration routine.

It had been quite a day. That afternoon Edie Adams and I were to meet Joan Sutherland backstage and then listen to her Los Angeles debut in *Lucia di Lammermoor*—an exciting plan. (Bing was in England, and it helped to fill in the time until he could return.)

My third baby wasn't due for three weeks, but in the morning I decided it might be sensible to go out to the doctor's for a routine examination. Mrs. Crosby came with me, and while waiting, I thought I'd take a swim with the children. The pool at Dotty's was warm and pleasant, though it was the twenty-ninth of October. The swimming coach dropped by, saying, "You know, Kathryn, I think Mary Frances is about ready for her Junior Red Cross test. It'll be kind of fun for her to be the youngest child ever to get one. She can do everything required, and she's just barely two."

"Let's see about it next week, Ginny."

"It doesn't look as if you'd be around next week."

"Little you know. Catherine Harrigan Crosby is going to be born in November. Doctor is just very cautious with me because when we were in England this summer at Cranbourne Court, I ate too much Devonshire cream. I'm afraid to weigh myself. I'm not merely pregnant—I'm fat."

Complacently I dozed by the pool while the water babies were splashing around playing tag underwater with Ginny and the Moss children.

What a summer it had been. A wretched beginning, because when Bing had told me he was going to England to school *Road to Hong Kong* with Bob Hope, I said, "Oh, that's great. When do we leave?" But he replied, "You don't. You're going to stay home and be with your children." Then, with an eye on my ample abdomen, he added, "You're in no condition to travel. It would be too much work for you to try to set up a house, particularly if you plan to bring over Harry or Mary Frances."

"Oh, but of course we have to take Harry and Mary Frances, darling. And I know how to find a house in England. You just look in the newspapers."

"No, dear, I'll be back in a month or two. You'll be much better off here with Mother."

I chewed a lot of nails behind closed doors during the next few days, then decided to say nothing more about it. Let him go to the end of the world. Let him go to the Arctic Circle—what did I care? I'd be pleasant, oh, so pleasant. I smiled, helped him get packed, even put luggage in the car for him.

Then Harry and I drove out to the airport to see Bing off. On the way out, Harry said, "Daddy, when can I come to England?" I pinched Harry, and he started to cry. He was just three, but he shouldn't say things like that.

Bing said, "Oh, I think in a week or so, old Buddy."

And I said, "Never mind, Harry. We've plenty to do here." We were nearing the airport and I became fascinated with the oil derricks on Signal Hill. Bing left—did he look just a mite guilty?

Twenty-four hours later the phone rang and Bing said, "Darling, I've looked at two places already. I should have us a place to stay in another day or two."

Well, it turned out to be Cranbourne Court, a splendid, typically English country house once owned by Lord Duveen, the great art authority. We were to share it with Bob and Dolores Hope and their children, and could Harry come with me?

"But," added Bing, "I'd like Mary Frances to stay at the ranch."

No problem. My sister, Frances Ruth, was delighted to have her up there, so Harry and I hurriedly packed for England.

What a summer it turned out to be! While Bing and Bob made their movie, Dolores and I and Father Brooks, a Jesuit, browsed through antique shops and drove around the English countryside and, one glorious occasion, we went with Tony and Linda Hope to the Continent. We were in Paris for a day or two, where I took my Louis XV tapestry chair covers to be rewoven. The whole transaction was in French. It turned out to be quite a charade. My first-year French was supplemented by a great deal of pointing and gesticulating. (I was glad I'd taken those courses in mime.) Somehow a meeting of the minds was achieved and a deal consummated, with lots of polite bowing by all concerned. Surprisingly, considering my inexperience, the chairs arrived on time and were perfect.

Then to Rome, where Dolores and I were allowed to hear Mass with Pope John XXIII, one of the first times responsive readings were used. Monsignor Ryan had arranged for us to be at Castel Gandolfo for this ceremony. I still cringe a little when I think of my first entry into the papal church. There were a few empty chairs to the left of the door, and because I was by then of conspicuous size and wearing a loose white linen coat, I wanted to sit down quickly—and did. Dolores snatched me to my feet.

Mother and Dad
with my brother Emery,
West Columbia, Texas

About to be
a Splash Day Princess,
age three

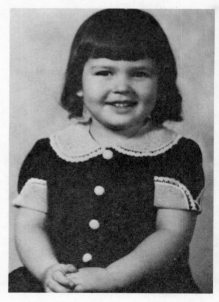

Miss Buccaneer Navy,
age fifteen
(Note skinned knees.)

Ball at Cabaniss Naval
Base, 1949

Above, Korea, Christmas, 1956

Right, Kathryn Grant in the
The Seventh Voyage of Sinbad

Left, On location,
Costa Brava, Spain, 1957,
with Kervin Mathews

The Grandstaff Family 1956; left to right, David Grandstaff, Emery, Dad, Me, Mother, Bill Meyer, and Frances.

With Bob and Dolores Hope, at Cranbourne Court,
England, 1961

Harry and I loved the garden at Cranbourne

At Greystoke, Cumberland, 1966, with Lady Lonsdale and
the Howards, and Bing as camera man

K.G.C. as Equestrienne,
Sussex, 1965

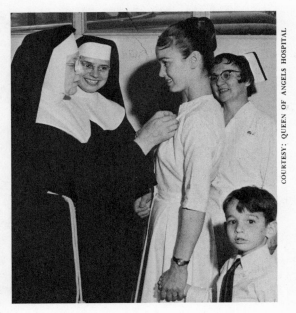

At Queen of Angels, receiving my pin

Dolores Milton, my
medical instructor,
supervises capping

Above, Bing's Fishing Cruiser, *Dorado,* off Las Cruces

Left, Bing's Amberjack: 60 lbs. of it

Below, After Mass: Las Cruces

Official Photo of Clams, 1964; back, left to right, Buster Collier, Ed Crowley, Bill Morrow, Dick Snideman, Buzz Fiorini; front, left to right, Phil Harris, Bing, George Rosenberg

The Hunting Wagon, Alabama, 1965

Bing and Remus
at Rising River

With Harry, Hollywood
Palace, 1965

I Imitate Mme.
Ouspenskaya, on
Ben Casey TV Show

LOOK MAGAZINE

"Last one in
is a rotten egg"

Nathaniel at
Hillsborough with
Bo, 1966

Mary Fran, First Communion,
with Well Wisher

Nathaniel's Fourth Birthday Party, with Daniel Boone

Alan Fisher and the children at Frontier Village, 1967

Right,
in *The Guardsman,*
Chicago, 1967

Below,
the Grandstaff Sisters
Model for Jean-Louis,
Palm Beach, 1967

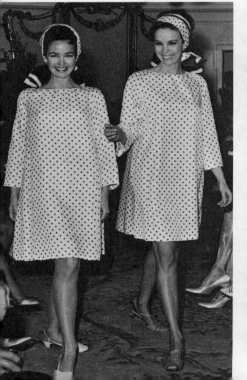

Your Friendly
Crooner, 1966

COURTESY: GABOR RONA

COURTESY: JOHN ENGSTEAD

A recent me

Our Hillsborough Home, Bing practicing

"Kathryn," she hissed, "that's the Cardinal's chair." I bolted, and we were marched into the proper pew where we sat by the Pope's sister. And such a beautiful Mass!

Afterward there was a harvest pageant. While the Pope sat on his throne, representatives of every region in Italy brought forward the produce of each area for blessing: hams, cheeses, wine, fruit. The Pope made a speech in three languages about love and abundance. Monsignor Ryan had tipped us off to watch his feet. I did and I noticed that he gestured with them as beautifully as he did with his hands. They scarcely touched the little fat pillow on which they were supposed to rest.

I laughed when he said in English, "I bless these things happily. I cannot eat them all. I would become too fat. Do you want to make me too fat?"

Then I thought back on our first audience with Pope John. Bing and I had been at Castel Gandolfo in 1960, and Pope John, after meeting Bing, asked, "Your mother had seven children?" When Bing confirmed this, the Pope quoted the warm homily: "The greater the oven to make the bread, the greater God's blessing on the family." And then he said, "Tell your mother the fourth decade of my rosary will be for her next Saturday evening." Of course we cabled mother to put her clock on Roman time.

When we got back to England, Bing told me several adventures that had occurred while we were away.

"You know, Kathryn," he said, "Bob and I worked out an arrangement with the others whereby we could quit work at five o'clock, hurry to Wentworth or Sunningdale and get in eleven or twelve holes of golf before coming back here to dinner. Well, last week, while you and Dolores were in Florence, we were shooting a scene in which the villains were giving us a farewell party because next day they were sending us to the moon in a rocket and to what they thought was certain death. Robert Morley was in charge of the villainy.

"So there we were in the midst of this bacchanalian revel, complete with dancing girls, flowing wine, and native music. I was stretched out on a couch being serenaded by some lovely Lorelei. Bob was on another couch with a couple of girls curling his hair, another pair plying him with wine and sweetmeats, one giving him a manicure, and still another painting his toenails red. Morley was looking properly sinister in the background. Things were humming when suddenly Bob looked at his watch. It was five o'clock. He flung the lovelies from him, upsetting the toenail enamel, called me, and we dressed hurriedly and raced for the golf course.

"We started our play in the long lovely English summer twilight, and later went to the locker room, the bleakest, most austere place you can imagine: just a nail to hang your coat on, a few benches scattered about, a washbasin in the corner with cold water for cleaning up. We were sitting side by side changing shoes and socks. Directly across from us there were two English gentlemen, Colonel Blimp types, with heavy tweed coats and luxurious moustaches.

"I looked up from tying my shoes and saw both of them staring in shocked disbelief at Bob's red toenails. They both looked at me as if seeking an explanation. I could only shrug my shoulders, whereupon one of the gentlemen said, 'Mr. Crosby, is your friend with the ballet?' Bob put on his socks, and, carrying his shoes, walked hurriedly to the parking lot without a word. It's the first time in our long friendship that I have ever seen Bob speechless."

Bing told the story in the lovely old dining room of Cranbourne Court, with ancestral portraits peering down from the walls. We enjoyed perfect service and marvelous meals there. Ascot was nearby, and we could go up to London to shop and lunch, or to the Old Vic to see *Romeo and Juliet*. I even tried to enroll in the Royal Academy of Dramatic Arts, but they weren't casting expectant mothers just then.

Then came the day a few weeks later when we tried to get me on a plane. Two airlines took one look and refused me transport, but a third finally decided that since I'd had nursing training, I might be staunch in an emergency and they agreed to book me. So Harry and I returned home.

Bing wouldn't be home for another two weeks, but he'd return in plenty of time to see the new baby born. There was really no hurry. At least that's what I thought until that lovely warm day by the pool when the contractions began and Dotty Moss and I rushed to the hospital.

Still, it was an old story for me. You had to fill out the forms— endless forms. Permit for surgery . . . permit for anesthesia . . . permit for circumcision (though *that* wouldn't be necessary because little girls don't need that sort of thing) . . . health insurance . . . signs and symptoms . . . first contractions . . . minutes apart . . . weight . . . blood pressure . . . I felt quite computerized when I got through with all those figures, but the adventure I was about to embark was far from machine-made. It could only happen to a woman.

A nurse's aide who had taught me did my prep. The enema came next. (I think they should figure out some way to do away with enemas.) Oh, I knew, they had taught us all about sterile fields and preventing contamination. I understood that the baby needed as much room as possible in the birth canal, just as it made sense that we weren't supposed to eat for six hours before childbirth because there was danger of food being inhaled during anesthesia.

"What did you last eat?"

"A peanut butter and jelly sandwich at noon."

"That Dr. Moss! How could he let you do that?"

"Don't you think it digests very quickly?"

"Come on, Kathryn, we'd better get you to bed."

I could only hope this session ahead wouldn't be as strenuous as Dotty's had been when Nannette Ellen had been born six months ago. Now Dot sat by me as I lumbered up on the table.

"You know, Dotty, I'm lucky to have you here. You're a good friend."

"Well, who rubbed my back for hours when I was carrying Nannette?"

"It was worth it. Look at Nannette. She's fine and healthy, even if you had contractions for nearly thirteen hours. And you were fine too—two hours later. I was the one who was exhausted. It was quite a night. Though I'd worked in Labor and Delivery, I'd never been with someone close to me during labor, and it just seemed to take forever. When I went down to the coffee room to see Dr. MacCarthy one time, the seventeen-year-old girl in the next room shrieked and I went in to talk with her for a minute. She had scopolamine flush. Her cheeks were so red, and she was so frightened. The side rails were up on her bed, but still there was an aide with her nearly all the time to keep her from thrashing around too much. The only good thing about her labor was that she wouldn't remember a bit of it.

"And then there was the Mexican woman in the next room who kept crying, '*Ay, ay!*' It was rhythmic and musical, not a scream or anything. I sat with her for a while and didn't even hear it, but you could hear it down the hall. Right next to her was the Oriental girl—beautiful, very young, and absolutely silent and motionless."

"That was one of Dr. Shigikawa's patients, wasn't it?"

"That's right. When Dr. Shigi's patient touched the call button for the first time, the nurses ran with the cart to get her to the delivery room. Her patients never move until the baby's ready."

"Stoic types," said Dorothy.

"There was a husband and wife, very sweet, in the next room. He wanted to go into the Delivery Room with her, but the doctor said No. At Queen's the husband can only stay in the Labor Room with his wife until she has anesthesia. The doctor told me why. One time they allowed a husband in the Delivery Room with his wife and she had a perfectly normal delivery. But when he saw the baby's head appear, he fainted, fell over backward, hit his head on the tile wall, and had a concussion. That ended that."

I looked at the clock on the wall. It was the same clock I'd carefully studied when Harry was born. The months before Harry's delivery had been so exciting, from the first affirmation by the doctor that I really was expecting, to the night when Bing and I had dinner at Chasen's with his agent, George Rosenberg, and I ate a butterfly steak and a chocolate soufflé, and felt that all was right with our world.

At two in the morning I wasn't quite so sure. I woke Bing, who drove me from West Los Angeles to Queen of Angels Hospital, a long, quiet way down Wilshire Boulevard. The streets were quite deserted, the street lights shone wanly through a light fog. There was a mystic feeling in the air. I felt that Bing and I were doing something no one else had ever done before.

Of course Dr. Moss had taken the wind out of my sails when he greeted us at Queens with, "Third sprout I've delivered tonight. Let's get with it, Kathryn." And to Bing's anxious query, "What should I do, Doctor? Stay in the coffee shop?"

"No, go on home and go to bed. Nothing ever happens when the husband stays around."

"Doctor," I asked him when he walked into the room, "why did you become a gynecologist and obstetrician?"

"Because, Kathryn, there are many mysteries in the world of medicine, but the most intriguing problems occur with women. Besides, I like kids."

Typical. Doctor would never stay serious for long. Maybe for a couple of sentences he'd play it straight, but then he'd digress— generally into a joke or a story. When a reporter asked if I were going to breast-feed, he came out with a typical Mossism. "Of course not. Breast-feeding is for women who live way out in the country and don't have neighbors."

Dotty blushed when I recalled it to her. "Originally," she told me, "he planned to say, 'It's great for the mother, but it doesn't do much for the kid.'" And she blushed again just thinking about it.

Sister Clement came in. "How are you doing, Mother?"

"Oh, Sister Clement, how nice to see you. I'm doing fine."

"Well, you're certainly not as much in a hurry this time as you were with Mary Frances."

"No, I'm getting to be an old hand."

When Mary Frances was born, I had only just had time to call Bing. He and George Rosenberg were deep in details concerning Bing's new movie, but when I gave him the alert, he left George with mouth agape and papers in his hand and bolted from the office. He picked me up at Dr. Moss's office and we drove down the Freeway. I must say Bing gave a poor performance that day of a man trying to look calm.

The prep then was very short and Bing sat in the room with me. Doctor was also present. The two men were discussing their kidney stones. Interesting, don't you think? Well, not to me, it wasn't, not just then. Men showed no solicitude for the Little Woman in Her Hour of Travail, I felt. There they were, gossiping like two old codgers: "Did you pass yours?" "No, they had to scope me." "What does your doctor let you eat?" "Oh, mine gives me certain things, but I don't follow any diet. Do you?" (This from a doctor himself!) On and on they went.

Finally the doctor said, "Let's speed this up a little," and inserted a syntocinon drip in my arm, whereupon I felt as if somebody had kicked me, hard, in the rear. I sat bolt upright and said, "Who did that?" And I realized that Mary Frances was about to make her debut in the world. She did—just twenty minutes later. I remember Dr. Moss shouting, "A girl! Bing's first little girl!" She had been terribly red and cried a lot.

And now our second little girl, Catherine Harrigan Crosby, was on her way. Obviously she wasn't going to be a very obedient child. I could tell that already because she was coming a month earlier than we had expected. No wonder the airlines hadn't wanted to sell me a ticket to return from Europe. And I began to think what it might have been like had it happened 35,000 feet above the Atlantic. Plenty of champagne and caviar for the others to celebrate with, anyway.

Suddenly I was aware I was back in Los Angeles, and almost down to sea level, but something *was* happening.

"Dotty, would you call Doctor."

She was holding my hand now. The contractions were only a minute apart. Doctor strode into the room and, after a quick examination, said, "Well, you're right. But why do you insist on presenting your babies sunny-side up?"

"This one too?"

"Yep. That's the third face presentation."

Just before the next contraction, Dr. Moss said, "Take a deep breath." I did. It seemed as if everything inside moved around. Then he was calling for the cart.

He explained blandly, "Rotation. It's really very simple."

Almost immediately we were in the Delivery Room and I remember Dotty holding my hand all the way there, her big brown
eyes serene and beaming encouragement. If only I could do as
well as she had done.

The next thing I heard was, "Weigh him again. I don't believe it."

Him? It must be a mistake. My dainty little delicate girl. I
asked, "Is she pretty?"

"It's a big fat slob of a boy weighing nine pounds two ounces,
and what in the world are you doing having a baby weighing nine
pounds and two ounces? The next time you lay off that Devonshire cream."

Then I saw the lovely big round boy. He looked as if he were
two weeks old already. I smiled at Dotty, and reached out my
hand to the doctor.

"Don't bother me, I'm busy. How can I do fine needlework
with females clutching at me."

I dozed off to happy slumber. Wasn't it wonderful—a healthy
baby girl—or rather, boy. Born in November. Or was it October? Obviously this one would have a personality all his own.

I lay in the bed at Queen of Angels Hospital—the place where
I'd worked so long, where I knew everybody, where I was going
to resume my nursing studies in February.

When Doctor came back that evening, I was cuddling the new
bit of still-red humanity. "Well, chum, let's see the animal.
What are you going to call him?"

"That's up to Bing. We had it all arranged for a girl, but he did
mention Nathaniel Patrick Crosby, if it was a boy. That would be
after his great-grandfather, a clipper-ship captain."

"Very nice. How do you feel?"

"I feel just great, Doctor. We've done it again."

CHAPTER 5

How To Become a Nurse the Hard Way

The alarm went off. I clutched for it wildly in the dark. Please don't let it wake Bing, please don't let it wake Bing! There—got it! Muffling it under the pillow, I found the button and pressed it down. Now, Hugh, our last rendezvous.

Quietly, stealthily, I sneaked to the door. The handle creaked as it turned, and I mentally vowed, as I had for weeks, to get some Three-in-One oil. The closing was an encore, and I heard a muttered imprecation from the bedroom.

Then into my dressing room. Five minutes later I was fixed for the day, and slipping downstairs in the dark. The waning rays of the moon, filtering through the French doors, lighted my way through the downstairs hall.

Lugging four great books in a tote bag, I lurched to the kitchen. In the icebox was my tray. The water for tea boiled quickly, the small steak was broiled in a matter of minutes, and I was deep in Medical-Surgical Nursing propped up on the newspaper stand. The steel-topped kitchen preparation table wasn't elegant for breakfast, but it served. Then a check to see that all the burners were off, and out to the car. I was off for the day.

I drove down Wilshire to Santa Monica Boulevard, then left at the fountain. I love that fountain at night—its lights change colors on sparkling waters.

Farther down Santa Monica Boulevard, the roadside park on the left atoned for the ugliness of the railroad tracks on the right. Then to the stoplight, and right on Beverly Boulevard—"Happy Street."

Dawn was coming up pretty fast now, and I checked my watch. Only six fifteen. I had plenty of time.

I had felt that Beverly Boulevard was "Happy Street" ever since I arrived in Los Angeles. I almost always managed to travel by this route. I liked to look in the windows of Herman Miller and Knapp and Tubbs, the decorators, closed to someone like me, but intriguing to the eye. Past La Cienega, Fairfax, and then the Farmer's Market. Early-morning produce trucks had just begun to bring in their wares, and I could see the peaches, Bing cherries, strawberries, and cantaloupes being delivered from outlying farms.

By instinct, listening to the Mexican radio station—KALI, *"Me voy lejos de tí—me voy muy lejos"* ("I am going farther from you . . . far, far away"), I veered right where Beverly crosses under the Freeway, and after a quick succession of turns, found myself in the maternity parking lot at 626 Coronado Terrace, Queen of Angels Hospital.

On the floor at 7:00 A.M., I became a proper student nurse—white shoes, white stockings, white uniform, white cap with a progressive number of blue velvet bands on the left wing tip. My hair was screwed up tightly under a net and four hairpins. The cap, which was held on by a comb sewn to the underside, fitted neatly over it.

Morning report was at seven o'clock sharp. Each patient in the area was discussed: changes in their condition; new doctor's orders; prescriptions to be refilled, continued or discontinued; patients requiring special attention from the staff. At 7:10 or 7:15, we were on our way.

I kept looking for seven basic needs, and trying to find ways to fill them. I sleepily recited to myself: Each patient, no matter what his or her condition, no matter what his medical problem, is a human being, and each human being has these needs:

1. A Need for Communication
2. A Need for Oxygenation
   a. Respiratory
   b. Circulatory
3. Fluids and Electrolites
4. Nutrition
5. Elimination
6. Activity and Rest
7. Comfort
   a. Physical
   b. Emotional

My first thought was of the doctor's chart, and whether I could discuss with the instructor why this patient had been chosen for me. After reading the report of the night nurse, and comparing it with my notes taken during the morning report, I began.

Breakfast would be up soon. Morning care must be given: hands and faces washed; water and emesis basin supplied for brushing teeth; urinal, bedpan, or a trip to the bathroom must be arranged; beds were to be straightened; and the environment must be made attractive before trays were passed out. And while all the physical needs were being met, I was looking, observing, watching, wondering.

This daily schedule had begun October 24, 1960, and was continued with interruptions until December 19, 1963. But within this daily schedule there was endless variety. The study plan was:

1. *First Year:* October 24, 1960–June 1, 1961
   a. Mother and Baby Care
   b. Nursery, Labor and Delivery
      Gynecology
      Pharmacology
      Community Health
2. *Second Year:* January 29, 1962–December 21, 1962
   a. Pediatrics
      Orthopedics
      Cerebral Palsy Clinic
      St. Elizabeth Day Nursery
      Premature Nursery

       Spadra
       Amputee Clinic
  b. Medical/Surgical Nursing
       Surgery
       Intensive Care Unit
       Emergency Nursing
3. *Third Year:* January 3, 1963—December 19, 1963
  a. Medical/Surgery
       Team Nursing
       Communicable Disease Nursing
       Clinic
  b. Psychiatric Nursing
       Team Leading
       Floor Nursing: Evenings
       Floor Nursing: Nights

Everything, even a nursing course, has its end, and on Thursday, December 19, I finished work on the floor, then walked across the driveway of the maternity entrance into the student cafeteria. I must have eaten thousands of peanut butter and jelly sandwiches there, and drunk a million cups of tea.

Mrs. Eva Stockonis, administrator of the School of Nursing, was waiting for me, and so were all my current classmates. In my jumping around I had studied with three different groups.

Now Dan Gann had his little flashbulbs going to record the historic event. Nathaniel, Mary Frances, and Harry were seated at one of the near tables to watch Mommy be graduated from her school.

Mrs. Stockonis who, through the years, had faced with me endless crises with wry good humor at the beginning ("All right, Kathryn, I suppose you don't have to live in the dormitories with the rest of the students. Just make out a request in triplicate to live at home with your husband and children."). Now she held in her hand that precious diploma—with seals and commendations.

She made a very pretty, quite amusing speech, recounting my entrance into the school and the travail we had all suffered since then. I've always loved the way Mrs. Stockonis garbled show business jargon to "improve our intrapersonal relationship." Well, I garbled nursing jargon just as badly.

"At first I was afraid," she told the students, "that this young woman was coming here for a publicity gag. She might have been using us just so she'd get a part on *Ben Casey* or *Dr. Kildare*." This drew a good laugh.

"And the first time she came into my office, she was wearing a mink jacket, and when she left with all her textbooks, I noticed that she was driving a brand-new 1957 Thunderbird."

I flushed at the memory. Her remark at the time had been, "Oh, Mrs. Crosby, are you sure you want to take up nursing?"

"And now you've earned your diploma from Queen of Angels. We wish you well. Congratulations."

I looked down on this tiny woman who had made me toe the mark for these last several years. I had been convinced on occasion that she was pitting her entire strength, and dynamic strength she had, against me. I had been morbidly obsessed with the fear that one slip and I would be out on my ear. Now I wanted to hug her. I looked at the table where the faculty was sitting. I thanked them all, gathered up my brood, and climbed into the Thunderbird, with Nathaniel strapped in on my side, and Harry and Mary Frances on the right seat.

The drive back down Beverly Boulevard was a slow one. Traffic was busy in the noon day, and there were lots of memories drifting through my mind.

The first meeting with Mrs. Stockonis had taken place at night, only two months after my marriage. Then followed two weeks of tutoring on bed making, pericare. Then Sister Timothy Marie, hospital administrator, asked if I would prefer to join the freshman class in the spring or work in surgery. I wanted to work in surgery, of course.

During the spring I had driven in from Palm Desert every week. I got to know my teachers. Bernice Milovic was one. Millie was always on a diet, and for good reason—she baked exquisite cakes and cookies for the coffee breaks. Then there was Madonna McGlone, a fiery, freckle-faced Irish girl. She taught me the duties of a circulating nurse. Rosemary Harris was a tall, beautiful dark girl with long, slender tapering fingers and a lovely smile. She was a scrub tech, and I worked with her on several surgeries. Sister Liguoria was the young head of Surgery. She taught me the instruments, the draping, and on my first visit shoved four books into my hands, saying "Memorize them!"

From that day to this, what a blur. How many chilling morning rings from my little alarm clock. I remembered my volunteer work with Dr. Haenel, a slight man with silver hair and a questioning countenance. His thick European accent made me think of Sid Caesar in one of his burlesques, as I followed him around St. Francis Hall, the psychiatric wing at Queen of Angels.

I took notes for him, was introduced to electrotherapy, made rounds, visited the patients on the floors, and received the first inkling that I might indeed be nurse material.

Sister Thomasine came into St. Francis Hall briefly during the weeks I was there, and said, "Kathryn, we consider you, while you're here, a nurse. The patient's identity as well as his care is in your safekeeping." I nodded, but I couldn't quite see the reason for this soft-spoken statement. Ten minutes later I understood. One of my husband's dearest friends was admitted. Bing never knew.

As we waited for the light at Western Avenue I thought, Oh, Hugh, did you really get me into this—nursing, I mean. For the first year or so, every instructor asked, "Why do you want to be a nurse?" Every teacher and doctor in the hospital, including the psychiatrist, asked why I wanted to become a nurse. I couldn't have told them about you. They'd have known I was crazy! I wonder, Hugh, if I'd even remember what you looked like now. I wonder if you have any recollection at all of the Paramount starlet who came to your bedside in the evacuation hospital in Seoul one sunshiny morning way back in April of 1953. Would you remember, Hugh?

I was Kathryn Grandstaff then, taking Dorothy Bromley's place as a girl from *Treasure Island,* the movie that Don Taylor and Audrey Dalton had made with Dorothy. It was to have its premiere in Seoul.

You never got to that premiere, Hugh. You'd been caught in a foxhole the night before, and had lost your left arm. I had been to hospitals before. I had seen my darling Uncle Leon slowly die of cancer. As a child I had seen grandmother die of undulant fever and felt morbid curiosity when Sandia, her Jersey cow, was shot and burned by the barn.

But I wasn't prepared for you, Hugh. You were just twenty. So handsome, so appealing with your brown curly hair fighting a crew cut. The instant we walked in the door, there you were. I gasped because the first thing I saw was your left arm stump suspended over a basket by some wire apparatus, dripping blood. I went to you quickly.

"Hello, I'm Kathryn Grandstaff. We came all the way from California just to say good morning to you."

You turned your head, and your eyes were glazed. You didn't look at me, you looked through me. Now I know that you were in shock, and probably still under anesthesia, but I didn't know that then. Then I just saw those dark eyes looking through me, unknowing, unseeing, uncaring.

I couldn't be flip or gay anymore, so I said, "Would you like me to stay, or would you like me to leave?"

You took my right hand in your right hand, Hugh, and you held it. You held it so tightly I thought bones were going to break. But I didn't care. I stayed with you for about ten minutes, just stayed with you, and when the Major told us it was time to leave, I kissed you good-bye. Do you remember?

I left the room slowly, glancing back at you; you were following me with your eyes now, and by the time we were outside in the tent having coffee with the nurses, I was filled with a rage—a rage I'd never felt before.

You had done all you could for your country, and what could I do? Hold your hand! That wasn't much. I saw Connie and the other nurses dressed in uniforms. They all had circles under their eyes from working eighteen hours a day. Their comfort stations were not private ladies' rooms, but an eight-hole outhouse with running water that came from a can hung on the wall. The shower bath was a twenty-five-gallon drum filled and tapped at will.

But these women were so alive, so full of purpose, of meaning. I knew then that some way, some day . . .

Connie was chatting on. "I wish you'd been here a little earlier, Kathryn. There was a Puerto Rican boy, a quadruple amputee. He was yearning for someone to speak Spanish with him."

I stammered out, "Oh, I'm sorry I wasn't here. I'd love to have met him." Quadruple amputee—no arms or legs!

Hugh, I could do something for you now. Now I know how to dress a wound such as you had. I know how to give sedatives. I could feed you now, and give you drinks of water without making you uncomfortable. I could put clean sheets on your bed without disturbing you or that suspension apparatus. I could bathe you and rub your back. And yes, somewhere in that eighteen-hour day, I could hold your hand. You carved such a place in my heart, Hugh, such a place in my life, and I only saw you those ten minutes. Never before—never again.

But this was for you, Hugh. Are you married now? And is your wife going to have a baby? I could sit with her while she's in labor, comfort her, observe her, prepare her for the doctor who would deliver your son or daughter. I could take that child and care for it, and tell you stories of my children, too.

I cared for hundreds of healthy babies, helped to deliver twins, but the day I'll never forget was in "preemy" nursery. A two-pound baby had been born at six and a half months' gestation. The nurses had been caring for it constantly, and since I was on double duty, they made me responsible for the infant. I was to watch it carefully and take care of no other babies that day.

The mite was so pitifully tiny, so obviously not ready to be born, that everyone despaired of its survival. It stopped breathing three times, but by manual resuscitation respiration was started again.

I suctioned, I watched, I waited. This baby was "mine" from seven in the morning until five in the afternoon, when inevitably it breathed its last. Part of me died with it. I wept bitterly. The nurses said, "Honey, it never had a chance. It was just too premature."

Then I filled out the death certificate. I had followed one human being on his entire mortal span.

Later we went to Spadra, the State Hospital for special children, and saw many babies who couldn't go to school or ever walk or talk—babies whose diagnosis was microcephalic, hydrocephalic, or Rh reaction.

You might take comfort from the sights we saw there. There was a beautiful little girl, just able to toddle around in a walker, with ringlets and big brown eyes and a very happy smile. What a pleasant child she was. She looked to be about a year and a half old, but the nurses in charge said she was seven. Her physical growth coincided almost exactly with her mental growth. And the love and care that she and her friends received at Spadra were exemplary.

Is there anyone in your family who found life too much of a pressure, so that they had to be committed? Some of the most rewarding work of my three years in nursing was at the Veterans' Hospital. There we were taught to care, really care, for each patient until he could begin to respect himself.

On my rotation there I was privileged to witness a miracle—not an uncommon occurrence in psychiatric nursing. A field trip was planned, not for the students but for the patients. The ones we worked with were chronic patients. That meant there was little hope for their recovery; they'd been in the hospital many years. They were signing up for a trip to Knott's Berry Farm. No one had to go, but there was great excitement and anticipation.

A handsome man of about fifty-five had been sitting in a corner, his very special corner, for almost twenty years. He wore no shoes, nor did he look at anyone, or speak. We were advised by our instructor that it would be unwise for us to come too close to him when we said good-morning, because he might feel threatened and think we were going to take his chair away from him. He felt great attachment for the chair.

But when the field trip to Knott's Berry Farm drew near, this patient asked to go. The orderly said, "Of course, but you'll have to wear shoes."

Two or three days later he said he thought he might wear shoes, and the whole department was soon in an uproar. They got the shoe shop to open. They took him over and fitted him with some that were a size too large, so his feet, which hadn't worn shoes for so many years, wouldn't be ruined by the walk.

The patients went down on a bus, about forty of them. I drove eight students and our instructor in the station wagon. There were so many exciting things to see. Panning for gold, the wax figures, the Old West decor, but I will never forget the sparkle in this man's eyes when he saw a little girl of about two. He just looked at her, then kneeled to touch her curly head. Her mother was right there, and I stood close to him and smiled at her. She never knew that he was a patient, and it was obvious that he wasn't going to hurt her baby. The two human beings, one very young and one weighted down with problems he could neither understand nor handle, looked at each other with absolute trust and confidence.

Two weeks later, at a round-table discussion (called "milieu therapy"), this man announced to the psychiatrist that he would like to go home. Whatever reasons he had had for sitting silent in a corner for twenty years had disappeared, apparently just because of his sunny day at Knott's Berry Farm.

Hugh, did you have brothers and sisters? I never really talked to you so I never knew, but I cared for a young girl who would have been just about the age of your sister—fourteen. She had rheumatic fever. And there was a boy with hair about the color of yours—chestnut brown. He had nephrosis, and would spend the rest of his life in a hospital. Then there was the boy with the broken leg. No one had ever read stories to him at home, and he was fascinated with Robert Louis Stevenson.

Did you ever have a girl friend? I cared for a girl with scoliasis, that strange sideway curvature of the spine. She was wearing a full body brace, and I learned to tip her from back to front, and let her rest on her side with no strain to her or to myself.

But I'm not a model nurse. I have serious problems that any GI might share. I suffer from insubordination, for one thing. One day in surgery, for instance, I thought I was pretty hot stuff as Number One Scrub for the Chief Resident, a doctor with tremendous skill with the knife. His tongue was just as sharp as his knife, a top-sergeant type. The other girls were scared of him, but I didn't spook easy.

The case started very well, and then the doctor began to suture, and my hand fumbled as usual and I dropped the needle and had to thread another.

"Okay, Crosby, give! I'll thread it."

I don't know what happened to me, but I turned on him and gave him a real freeze job. "Please don't embarrass me any more than I am embarrassed already." Then I threaded the needle and handed it over. "Closing suture, Doctor."

For one half second I thought the fierce surgeon would order me out of the Operating Room. Not so. He gave a faint half-smile, took the needle and said, "Now you're learning, Crosby. Just get a little more speed to it."

And combat fatigue! There were days and nights when I was afraid to stop moving because I knew I'd fall asleep standing, sitting, or lying down.

But anyway, I learned to do these things for you, Hugh. It's to say "Thank you" for what you did for me.

Now the cars were honking behind me. The light had changed twice since we'd stopped. Harry was saying demandingly, "Mother, are you ill?" Mary Frances chimed in, "May I take your pulse?"

"No, I'm fine. Just fine."

Bing, that evening, congratulated me warmly and then, sobering, he said, "Well, now there's a little thing called the State Board exam. Do you really think you can pass it?"

"Of course."

"You won't take it until March 10 or 11. That's months from now. There'll be Christmas, and then we're going down to Las Cruces, and you know it's pretty hard to study while you're looking for marlin. And Fran and Bill are coming out from Piqua and we're going to do a lot of dove shooting."

"Are you insinuating that I can't pass the Board?"

"Not insinuating, dear, just saying it's quite a while since you studied and you'll be rusty. And actually you've gone at this so erratically, so many breaks between semesters, I just don't see how it's possible for you to pass it. You weren't the ideal nurse, you know."

"Would you, dear, like to back your skepticism with a sizable bet?"

"Well, I didn't mean to awaken the gambler that lurks in your Baptist soul, but I suppose I could find a little change in my pocket."

"I'm not interested in change. I'll bet a trip to Tierra del Fuego against a chunk of Fabergé. A flower, maybe."

"We will consider this a wager, Mrs. C. And now, do you think it will be possible for me to have some unbroken morning sleep for a change?"

"Oh, did I wake you?" I said with huge naïveté.

"Only every morning for the last five years . . ." He fixed me with one of those unyielding blue gazes, then smiled, refilling his pipe, and said, "Tell me, did you achieve your purpose, reach your goal? Will Hugh be satisfied?"

"Hugh! How do you know about him?"

"You talk in your sleep, particularly before exams. Something about Korea, wasn't it?"

"Yes." I started to feel rather strange and small.

"You never forget experiences such as those. I can still remember the days I spent in Europe during World War II. The troops worn, muddy, the walking wounded, the field hospitals every night, the sacrifices some of them made. Makes anyone feel a deep sense of obligation."

"And you know, the strange thing, darling, is that even though I tried to pay a debt of gratitude, it just grows bigger. Now I'm so much more confident with the children and your mother."

"Perhaps even overconfident where State Board exams are concerned." He puffed on his pipe, sending a thin mist of ash over the rug, one of his ways of laughing. "However, just don't come at me with one of those needles of yours—not even an aspirin tablet."

A few months later in San Francisco—I was all dressed up for the opening of the opera in a new Jean-Louis gown and long gloves, and Bing looked smashing in his white tie and tails—he shouted to me from the bedroom, "Kathryn, come here. You really must get these vitrines moved—perhaps to this wall."

I couldn't imagine what inspired such domestic concern. Bing had just come up from Los Angeles, we were ready to leave. . . . Then I saw, but I couldn't believe it! Not the one flower, according to our wager, but three: a crystal pot with seven cornflowers; a small urn with lilies of the valley; a viburnum bush growing out of gold dust. Yes, I'd passed the State Board . . . *magna cum laude,* it seemed.

"Oh, darling! I'll be your special nurse forever!"

"Don't be so commercial," he growled.

CHAPTER *6*

How To Have a Career or Two

This was the day. What a day it was to be! I slid out of bed and looked at my nursing watch, the automatic watch that Bing had given me on our first anniversary. "Happy First" was engraved on the back of it, and though I slept so soundly that it would often lose time during the night, I glanced at it and knew that I was running late.

The house was silent now—nobody up yet, and the children had to be gotten off to school. I skinned my hair back in a ponytail and grabbed a robe, trying to tiptoe and run at the same time. Down the backstairs.

I put the kettle on and then donned a big plastic apron that would handle all the complications that were bound to arise before breakfast was finished. I set the table quickly, only forgetting two forks. Got the eggs, put the bacon under the broiler, put the hot cereal on to cook, stirred in a few raisins, and then sneaked off to my office.

There on the top shelf was his gift, in a black leather box hidden carefully behind Appleton-Century's *A Gallery of Flowers.* I took it into the library, which was where I thought I'd make my presentation. I opened it and peeked. David Webb had created a bed of anemones from tiny turquoise beads with gold spines nestling on a rock of blue and green with gold seaweed growing up from the base. If you squinted, it looked like something you'd see under the water at Las Cruces. Yes, Bing would love this.

I closed the box and ran back to the kitchen. There was Bing getting his first cup of coffee. "Good morning, darling." I started to give him a hug.

"Watch it. My shoulder hurts a little this morning."

I backed up, a little miffed. "Do you know what day this is?"

"It's Monday. All day!"

"Yes it is, Monday, October 24." I began to scramble eggs furiously.

Harry came running down the stairs. "Mother, Nathaniel Patrick is not getting dressed."

I whirled on him. "You go right back up there. Help him get dressed and both of you make your beds."

"Oh Mom, he's no help at all."

"Do as I say."

Harry marched up the stairs. About that time Mary Frances came down with her hair looking like a basket of snakes. "All right, Mary Frances! Get the brush and the tail comb and work out those snarls. I'll do your French braid right after breakfast. And be sure you wash the sleep out of those eyes."

The children ate quickly and with acceptable manners. This was not a day to bother Mother.

Nathaniel grinned, "You see, Mom, I beat."

"More eating, less talking—it works every time. Congratulations, Nathaniel. You're President of the Clean Plate Club."

We ran down and caught the bus at the gate just as it arrived at eight thirty. I was very careful to hide behind the hedge because the children didn't think I should be seen in the street in a robe.

Then all the starch went out of me. How could Bing forget this day? I knew I should go upstairs and get dressed quickly, make the beds, put on lipstick, and do my hair up in that horrible severe bun that only took thirty seconds to achieve. I didn't care. He wasn't worth it!

I walked into the library. "May I have a talk with you?"

Bing was right in the middle of Jim Murray's column, but he

put down the sports page and looked at me solemnly. He must have divined the seriousness of my intent.

"Bing, we're beginning our tenth year of marriage now. What do you want of me? How can I best serve you?"

He had a ready response. "I want you to stay home and raise your children."

"Well, I didn't have them all by myself. And don't you think I'd be a horribly dull *Hausfrau?*"

"I don't know," he responded with a glint in his eye. "Try it and we'll see."

"Now look, Bing, the children learn to play from you—baseball, football, games. The afternoons when you walk over to Fagan's and have the softball games are the greatest fun for them. They love to travel with you, and Harry adores going to the club with you, and fishing. They know a little about the fun of your kind of work, like when you do the Hollywood Palace, and I'm sure visiting you on the set of *Robin and the Seven Hoods,* when you sang 'Don't Be a Do-Badder,' and on location at *Stagecoach* was instructive. Surely they gain from you, but don't you think they've gained something from going on my theater jaunts with me?"

"Yes, if we're raising gypsies. But the most important things they're going to gain from you are right here in their own home."

"Oh, but darling, Chicago was such a rich experience for all of us. *Arms and the Man* is a beautiful play, and the South Shore Country Club a marvelous place for children, right on the lake, where they could play in the sun every day and meet new friends. And then there were Debbie and Chi-Chi DeSantis, the producer's children. They were grown girls, wonderful with our kids. And with my mother along, it was just great. She held school every morning, and Mary Frances did all her first-grade work in just six weeks. And I think they profited by going to work with me every night. Why, Nathaniel Patrick Crosby, at only three years of age, could quote Shaw."

Bing said wryly, "I consider 'Cease firing, damn it' neither particularly Shavian, nor highly educational for a three-year-old.

And dragging those youngsters through the lobby of the Drury Lane every night in their pajamas at eleven P.M. Madness!"

"They were supposed to sleep in my offstage dressing room, only Mom used to let them watch the play. And think of the business experience Harry gained—working the cash register for Mrs. DeSantis."

"He broke it."

"Well, then he went to Colorado with you. That was fantastic for him, and during that time Mary Frances worked furiously on her reading. And then she went fishing with you. How many little girls get to go off with their daddy for two weeks in Colorado?"

"Yes," Bing melted, "she looked like a princess when she arrived. Her French braid was so pretty with the bow at the bottom. And she tripped along like a real young lady in her crisp cotton dress with her shoes polished, and her socks neatly turned down."

I was piqued at this frivolity and interposed, "When she returned two weeks later she looked as if she'd come down a chimney backward with the shoes on the wrong feet, and no socks at all. Eggs, jelly and milk from the plane breakfast all over her blue dress, her nose peeling, and her hair! Oh, dear, honey, I've got to give you a course in French braiding before she goes off with you again."

"I'll get her a page-boy wig, but I tell you one thing: This gal will always get along. She's so outgoing and gregarious and poised. She's been that way since she's been a toddler. I'm sure if ever there's a need for another Carrie Nation, or Amelia Pankhurst, she can adequately qualify."

"Sister William at Immaculate Heart College says she's going to enter the Order as Mother General."

"Did I tell you about her in *Black Lake?*"

"I don't know. What did she do this time?"

"Well, we had a couple of days off the picture and I took her up with me to visit Dave Chasen and Maud high up in the mountains. Buster and Stevie Collier and a Mr. and Mrs. Hanson were there. They're my age, you know. But Mary Frances fitted in perfectly. After we arrived, there was a cocktail party. When everyone had sat down with their drinks, Mary Frances popped up and said, 'Would anyone like me to sing?'

"Silence fell on the group, but that didn't deter her at all. 'What would you like me to sing?' she asked.

" 'Anything you want,' encouraged Stevie.

" 'Well, you see,' she said, 'I make up all my own songs. What would you like me to make up one about?'

"Someone suggested the lake, so she broke into a seemingly endless number about the lake, its depth, its color, and its temperature. She then did one about the birds, and another about the boats, and one about the tall pines, and then she said, 'Would you like me to do one in Spanish?'

"By now she owned them, so they could do little but acquiesce. And with her four words in Spanish, she came up with something that would have killed 'em in Acapulco.

"She fished with Dave that evening, and then again the next morning. She took over the netting of the fish, and in the meantime maintained an incessant flow of conversation."

"Oh, no!"

"But the ladies were her game. She never failed to compliment them on their gowns, their hairdos, their tans, their shoes, or their jewelry. She won a lot of points with this kind of ploy. When it came time to leave, Maud, Mrs. Hanson, and Stevie were going into the village, so we drove out at the same time. When we came to the fork in the road where they went north and we went south, both cars stopped, and we said good-bye. Just as we drove off, Mary Frances stuck her head out of the window, waved her hand, and cried gaily, 'Good-bye, all you lovely girls.' "

We sat quietly for awhile, smiling, all the early rancor gone, thinking of our funny grown-up little girl daughter. Then I remembered the very personal reason why I loved my "career."

Chicago was a great place to work, but its attractions were enhanced when Bing came into town to visit me. This time he'd been in New York and bought, as a surprise, for no reason, a glorious small agate box which had been used for cigarettes by someone at the Czar's Court. It was just the right size for an evening catchall for me. It would hold my contact lenses and a handkerchief, all I ever carried in the evening. For him to realize that, and think of it, and bring me this precious *objet d'art* . . . He knew of the ridiculous fascination Fabergé held for me, and that I used to press my nose against the glass of A La Vieille Russie in New York when I was doing public appearance tours for Columbia Pictures . . . how I finally got nerve enough to go in and meet Mme. Segé, a tall, handsome woman who showed me everything in the store, knowing from the start that I couldn't possibly buy anything.

My first purchase had been a letter opener of jade for Bing, and a tiny little mushroom tie tack which I used as a lapel pin. And now this summer in Chicago he'd brought me that gift to say, "Good show." He tossed off his generous gesture, saying, "It looks like something 'Raina' would have, don't you think?" He even saw the show twice, so he must have thought my performance acceptable.

One day the two of us sneaked off to the art museum to be enchanted by Seurat's "A Sunday Afternoon on the Island of La Grande Jatte," and the Renoir picture of the babies with oranges. Then we had a very fine lunch, just the two of us, at the small dining room in the Drake, with caviar and Chablis. What a lovely afternoon. I felt almost clandestine.

And there was the year before, when Bing had come to Holyoke, Massachusetts, at the end of my tour with *Sabrina Fair*. The weather was foul, and his plane had made three passes at the field before it could land. The state police escorted him with all ceremony to the theater. He was mobbed, of course, between intermissions. But when the show was closed, we got Mother off safely for Texas, drove through Connecticut, visited Bing's brother at his farm in Salisbury, and then went to New York for four days of going to plays and seeing the city. Just the two of us.

We saw the famous Christie Fabergé collection at the Metropolitan Museum. One day while we were walking along Fifth Avenue, a passing pigeon blithely spattered the front of his topcoat. He shook his fist at the sky and muttered, "Critic!"

And the year before that, when I'd started my play career, how worried he was about my being able to do a show at all. I had grave doubts myself, but he was so concerned about how I would be received that he called our dear friends, Betty and Bruz Ruckelshaus, and mentioned that I was going to open at Avondale Theatre in Indianapolis, where they lived, in *Sunday in New York*. Betty naturally said, "But Kathryn must stay with me, and we'll pack the house with ardent supporters."

The opening at Avondale was a near disaster. A violent rainstorm hit us, and there was a power failure. In many ways the disturbance made my debut hysterically funny. We had to do parts of Act I three times, Act II was done in total darkness, and by the middle of Act III the tent began to leak. But none of the audience left. We were sloshing about the stage relentlessly, but the audience had good humor, and I had fun. Bing finally came to see the show with Harry in Warren, Ohio.

Bing interrupted my reverie. "All right, so Chicago was not a bad experience for the children; but what about last summer? We were in Las Cruces, everything serene, everybody happy, until suddenly you went into an absolute snit, and then you left your family for five weeks. What mother in her right mind would do that?"

"Well, if it had been you waiting for a script, Leo Lynn would have chartered a jet to get it to you. But for me, he simply sent a note that 'mail would proceed with the fresh artichokes,' which I assumed he was picking himself. I had exactly two days to learn *Mary, Mary*. All right, it's possible, but it's not possible to characterize the role much, especially when I had to vaccinate fifty Mexican youngsters that last day. And in the second place, I wanted to take the children and you wouldn't let me."

"I should say not—lurching around the country like gypsies. They need to be home with their parents."

"Oh, is that what they were doing when you took Harry off to Hawaii for two weeks?"

"I thought he should learn to surf, and besides, I'd agreed to play in that charity golf tournament."

"Of course, it was good for him, Bing. I'm not grudging him or you any of that, and don't think my mother and dad didn't have fun with me meanwhile. Daughters have responsibilities that way too, you know. They saw Vineland, Ontario, and we had our first clambake at the Lakes region, and we went antiquing in Ivoryton, Connecticut, and they saw Boston when we were at Fitchburg. And then at Falmouth they were able to meet Mrs. Joseph Kennedy. And Mrs. Kennedy told me not to do too much for the children because it weakens them. I suppose she's right—she has quite a record as a mother."

"So has your mother. To let you grow up without strangling you showed great restraint on her part."

"She saved me for you, dear. I'll tell you about my mother. She believes that each child is a very special human being with infinite capacities. She guided us by two truisms. One: Do the best you can; two: You can do anything you have to."

"Seems to me you try to do a lot more than you have to. That nursing course, for instance. Five years of irregular hours. You kept us all upset, disrupting the whole family schedule."

"I am not practicing in San Francisco, my dear. I know I couldn't make a seven-to-three shift, or a three-to-eleven shift, or an eleven-to-seven shift, so I'm content to limit my practice for the time being to Las Cruces."

"Yes, you've developed some needle-shy Mexicans down there. They say '*Buenos días*' to you, and you hit 'em with an injection."

"It's good for 'em. Who was it that volunteered me to be on the Board of Directors for the Dwight D. Eisenhower Memorial Hospital?"

"That's important. But really now, do you have to model for Jean-Louis too? I honestly think it's entirely unnecessary for you to be prancing and capering about that way for a clutch of buyers."

"Oh, but that's not all I do. Jean just designs the clothes on me then. But you insist we do the Heart Show in Palm Beach, the Swan Ball for your friends in Nashville, and the Pittsburgh Symphony Benefit. Frances Ruth does the Reno Heart Show and you, just last year, volunteered me for the hospital benefit show in Carmel for Ginny Stanton."

"Ginny's hard to shake. But anyway, a well-organized charity show which is capable of producing a substantial sum for worthy

causes, that's different. It's worth your time—even though inevitably you'll get carried away and buy a few gimps and dirndls."

"But what I really don't understand is your current objection to
my teaching."

"No genuine objection. It's just that you have so many other
things: your children, a house to run, this book you're writing—
and even, sporadically, a husband to please," he said plaintively.

"But I've explained to you, Bing. I just got the credentials—
the elementary and the secondary—and if, for instance, you go on
location in Europe, I'm qualified to teach our children. But I have
to prove to myself that I'm capable of handling the education of
our offspring to your satisfaction, to mine, and to the satisfaction
of the State of California. It's challenging work. And it's not as
if I were teaching every day. I'm only on the substitute list."

"Kathryn, honestly, I applaud your zeal. I heartily approve your
substituting. But must you time it so that when Alan and Norma
Fisher are off on their five-week holiday to Europe, and our
house is full of house guests, you have to teach? Why don't you
take up some household enterprises? Replace a few light bulbs,
clean out the garage, get the clock fixed, mop the kitchen floor."

"You saw me just last week spend fourteen hours of my time
and Monica's—Monica with her college diploma in nutrition—
pounding out grapes—four crates of grapes—and making what
Monica called a big chemistry experiment. Too bad it didn't jell
at all."

"Yes, yes. That was a clever caper."

"Well anyway, we got the floors polished the other day, even
though we had to do it twice. How was I to know you must use
long, flowing strokes or it shines up like a floor with a permanent
wave?"

"Oh yes, dear, you have sudden bursts of great energy that last
about half a day, then you fall down exhausted."

"So I'm a flop around the house?"

"You are not a flop. You simply try too much. If you'd concentrate on one thing at a time, you'd be all right. But you book four
things for the same time, and then go into a tailspin and cry for
help. 'Help! Help! Help!' You," he continued, "have a pathological

incapacity to say No. If the Little Player's Theatre of Split Lip, Nevada, called and said they wanted you for a role, you'd drop everything and fly."

"Did they call?" I gasped eagerly.

"No," he said in disgust.

"You don't even mention my summer session at the University of Texas? I didn't consider being a guest professor an honor to be taken lightly, and I thought you'd approve of my playing in *Pygmalion* coached by B. Iden Payne and under the direction of James Moll. We filled Hogg Auditorium for three nights."

Bing looked at me briefly, and then resumed Jim Murray's sports column, after which he switched to the *London Times* to study the racing section. I just sat there and stewed. Could I never do anything right? I remembered his letter, received in Chicago:

Dearest,

I just finished playing Mary Martin's *Peter Pan* album. Much as I dislike throwing cold water on your hopeful zeal, I must be real sadistic and tell you that I doubt very much if you can carry this off. You must remember that these songs were written for Mary. One of the finest singers the musical comedy stage has ever seen. . . .

We live in San Francisco now, and I can think of nothing more crushing than to have this thing come off badly. I would not like to move again. . . . I can be wrong. I haven't heard you sing the songs. Maybe you can do them. Do you think you can? Would you sing them for me?

I had called Max Arnow immediately and said, "Max, see if you can get me out of the contract. Bing doesn't think I can do it."

"Well, Mrs. Crosby," said my agent, friend, director of talents, and supervisor for many years, "I think you can do it. But finish what you're doing in Chicago. Work with a piano player. Come back here and audition for him."

"Audition for him! I've lived with him for eight years. If he doesn't think I can sing, he should know. I wouldn't sing for him for all the Fabergé flowers in the world."

But I did. The Hyatt House was cold at two o'clock in the afternoon. Nobody was in the theater—well, almost nobody. There was a man in a sports coat and a hunting cap. There was a producer—Herb Rogers. There was the orchestra conductor, Joseph Klein, who was going to play piano, and there was I, an aspiring Peter Pan.

I walked down the aisle to the orchestra pit and my knees were weak. What right had I to be here? Absolutely none in the world. How had Max Arnow persuaded me to change my mind?

"How do you do. I'm Kathryn Crosby."

"I'm Joseph Klein," the confident young man responded.

"Now, I have these keys I rehearsed in in Chicago. You might want to look at them."

He played a few chords. "Does this sound about right?"

"Oh, that's fine." I glanced up and at the back of the theater saw a curl of smoke coming from a pipe. I climbed up the stairs out of the pit and walked onto the large stage, looking out into the darkened theater.

> I have a place where dreams are born
> And time is never planned.
> It's not on any chart;
> You must find it with your heart—
> Never Never Land

Here was my never-never land. The stage—the theater. Cold and empty, it still held such magic for me that I couldn't resist knowing that these few feet of space were mine to share, mine to give. No, I couldn't sing, but I could tell a story.

> It may be way beyond the moon
> Or right there where you stand.
> Just keep an open mind,
> And suddenly you find
> Never Never Land.

I finished the song. The two gentlemen conferred briefly. The man in the sports coat stood up and moved forward. "All right, honey, you win. Your zeal is infectious, and you *are* loud enough. Yes, I think you can get away with it."

All I could find to say was "Thanks." *Peter Pan* was more than a two-week Christmas run at the Hyatt House. It became a way of life. It threatened to overthrow the whole Crosby regime.

Mary Frances played the part of Jane, a vignette that has four or five lines at the end of the show. She surpassed all my fondest expectations. She even covered for me once when I dropped a line, ad libbing and carrying on gleefully. She loved the flying. And our friends were nearly always in tears when they came backstage and said, "The sight of you and that little cherub flying off into never-never land was more than I could bear."

But I'd expected that of Mary Frances. What I hadn't counted on was Harry and Nathaniel. Nathaniel said, "Mother, if Mary Frances is going to be Jane, I want to be Captain Hook."

"That's fine, darling, and you can at home. But you must get to be a lot taller to play Captain Hook on the stage because there's the big sword fight, you remember. And besides, Mr. Michael Evans has already been invited to do the show and accepted, and we wouldn't like to call him back and tell him to go home."

Nathaniel, then a sage of four, said, "Maybe when I'm five?"

Harry quietly asked, "Mother, how old does John have to be?"

"Oh, I suppose John is a boy your age—about seven. But he's probably played by a boy who is at least twelve because it's a very big part. Last summer, when I did the show in Indianapolis, you remember—when I visited Aunt Betty and Uncle Bruz and Bettina played an Indian Brave with me—well, that summer it was played by a boy who was twenty-one, even though he was short."

Harry said, "I see. Then what about Michael?"

I responded not so adroitly this time, "Well, Michael is probably Nathaniel's age, really, but he's usually played by a boy about your age—possibly a little bit older because Michael has a very important part to play. He has all those lines. He works all through the show."

Harry stepped forward confidently. "I'd like to play Michael."

"You would?"

"Yes, I would."

"Well, you'll have to try out with all the other boys."

"That's all right."

"Okay. You go and play for a little while and I'll see what I can do." I thought Harry would forget all about it.

Around noon he came in and said, "Mom, where's your script? I want to look at my lines."

So we read the lines, and Harry, who hadn't been 'motivated' at school (meaning he was lazy) started reading his lines, and not only reading them, but doing it very well. We acted out several of the scenes, and then I picked out with one finger "Tender Shepherd," which is the song the children sing at night.

Next day at dance rehearsal I retold what had transpired and asked if it would be all right for Harry to try out. It would be a good experience for him whether he was right for it or not, and he could certainly learn a little bit more about show business.

Mr. Rogers agreed. "Sure. We're having auditions next Thursday."

Home from dance rehearsal. I went to Bing and said, "Darling, Harry wants to be Michael, and he's worked on the part, and he's going to try out next Thursday."

Bing retorted, "Oh, I don't think so."

"But why?"

"Because we're going shooting during Christmas vacation. He's going to have a holiday with his father. I don't want to lose all my family to the theater."

"But don't you see, Mary Frances has been given a part in the show. If he *earns* the part, he'll have a sense of accomplishment." I didn't convince Bing.

"Are you sure you haven't cajoled him into something? Let me talk to him later."

I did a little double-checking. Mr. Brown, the principal of the school, thought it would be fine for Harry to try out for the role, but not necessarily for him to win it. Mrs. Haderer, his teacher, knowing what a sensitive boy Harry was, wondered what would happen if he failed. Mrs. Smegel, Mary Frances's teacher, and I agreed that it would be the best thing in the world for both Harry and Mary Frances if he got the role in *Peter Pan*. Dr. Kokjer, the school psychiatrist, mused, "You've got a problem there."

The conversation between Bing and Harry in the office was hysterical. I know because I eavesdropped a little. Bing led off with, "Son, I understand you want to try out for *Peter Pan*."

"Yes, sir, I do."

"You sure your mother didn't talk you into it?"

"No, sir. I want to try out."

"Why?"

"Because I want to be Michael."

"Do you want to be Michael just because Mary Frances is Jane?"

"Well, maybe so, but I want to be Michael too."

"Don't you realize you'll have to spend every day of Christmas studying and doing lines, and then doing the show in the afternoon, and then staying up all night?"

"Oh, I'd love to stay up all night."

"No, what I mean is . . . you'll have to be studying all the time when you and I could be out fishing for stripers or going up to the ranch to see about those geese and ducks up there, and visiting with Uncle Leonard and riding the horses."

"Oh Dad, really!"

"And just between you and me, son, maybe Mr. Vanoff would like you on the Hollywood Palace."

"The Hollywood Palace! Cooool! That's better than anything Mom does."

"Shhh—not so loud!"

Then they opened the door quickly and caught me red-faced in the corridor.

"Dad, I'd still like to try out for the part."

"All right, you can try out for the part."

Later Bing said to me, "It's all right for him to read, but he can't play Michael. One of them seems enough." And that was that.

I took Harry over to the stage, but somehow I couldn't tell Mr. Klein and Mr. Rogers that this wasn't a real test. I just said, "Good luck, darling," and sent him down the aisle.

There were fifteen or twenty boys on the stage and Harry went up and sat with them. Suddenly I wasn't Peter Pan anymore. I was just a mother—any mother hoping that her child does well.

The director said, "All right, young man, what's your name?"

"Freddie Spencer."

"Would you sing a song for me?"

"Yes, sir."

Then out came a little quavering rendition of "Happy Birthday" accompanied by the piano.

The next young man stood up. "What is your name?"

"Milton Hirsch."

"Will you sing a song for me?"

"Yes."

"What can you sing?"

"I can sing 'Happy Birthday' all right."

"Fine."

So he sang "Happy Birthday," but it wasn't quite all right. It was a little flat.

The next young man stood up very straight, I thought, and said, "My name is Harry Crosby, and I'd like to sing, 'Tender Shepherd.'"

Mr. Klein smiled, raised his eyebrows, and said, "Oh, you would, would you?"

The accompanist started the introduction. Harry turned and said, "That's not the way you play it. My Mom picks it out with one finger." So the accompanist picked it out with one finger and Harry sang "Tender Shepherd" in a pure boy soprano—sweeter to me than the soloist in the Vienna Boys' Choir. I was crying unbashedly—safe in the dark shadows in the rear of the auditorium. Other mothers were looking at me muttering, ". . . fixed" to themselves.

Mary Frances, all the while, was sitting on the stage near her brother fidgeting and waiting impatiently to sing. When they didn't ask her, she volunteered to Mr. Rogers, "I can sing," and while Harry did some line readings in Mr. Rogers' office, we could hear

Mary Frances shouting, "I won't grow up" to all the secretaries outside.

The next day I called Mr. Klein and asked, rather proudly, "How did Harry do?"

"He was fine. Herb and I think we'd like him for the part."

"Oh, that's so nice, but Bing says Harry's going to be on the Hollywood Palace, and the rehearsal times would interfere."

During the Christmas season, since Bing's show was taped early, Harry and Mary Frances kept a running dialogue. Mary Frances would say, "Well, I must get ready, Harry. Mother and I must go over to the theater to do our show."

Harry: "I've already done my show. It's going to be the 'Christmas Bing Crosby Hollywood Palace Show,' also starring Harry Crosby."

"Yes, but we do a show every day for two thousand people."

"That's okay. Four million, billion, zillion people see Daddy's and my show."

Nathaniel put in plaintively, "Mommy, when am I going to be tall enough to be Captain Hook?"

And for months after that, never-never land was the lullaby of the evening.

I was staring fixedly at Bing, who slowly lowered his paper and looked at me. "Well?" he asked.

"I was just thinking. I don't play golf four hours every day. I don't say I'm home for the next couple of weeks and then go into San Francisco and have lunch with the fellows at noon, returning just in time for dinner. There are weeks when I don't leave the house at all. There are days when I can't even answer the telephone, I'm so busy cooking and cleaning and packing Christmas presents for your thirty-two godchildren. There are many evenings when you're watching television and I'm up in the schoolroom teaching."

"Yes, that's another thing. You're really much too strict on the children. They get enough schoolwork at school, and then you've got them—Harry in gymnastics and guitar lessons, and Mary

Frances in ballet, and they have piano lessons after school, and catechism during the week. Why, they're exhausted by evening."

"Now look, dear. You hate bad children just as much as I do. As far as our three are concerned, we love them because the Lord gave them to us and we have to love them, but nobody else does. And if they're not well-trained children, if they're not nice and disciplined, precious few will. It's not fair to send a child out in the world with no preparation. He's got to make his way. And as far as you're concerned, you won't take them to dinner if they don't have decent table manners, and I think it's much nicer for them to be spanked and get proper manners than not to be spanked and to be left at home when you want to go out to supper. Which is the worst punishment?

"I know I'm tough on them, and I'll tell you when I'm mostly tough on them. I'm tough on them when I feel you don't love me. Like when I've had your anniversary gift since last summer, and you can't even remember what day it is. Then I'm apt to be unfair to the children. I cannot bear it when you get Irish and quiet and don't want me around. And I know, Bing, I know I don't wear well. There are days when I can't bear myself." And I started to cry.

"Kathryn, you should know I love you. It's part of me. I don't say it often. I feel awkward and graceless, but it's there."

His eyes were so blue and deep, not icy now, not merry. He took my face in his hand and planted a kiss firmly—a very hard feat because I was crying so hard and my face was slippery. His whiskers burned, and I clung to him and sobbed. "I'm so sorry. I guess I just like to be dragged back to the cave. That's why I wanted to do that movie in Hong Kong—to lure you to the Orient after me. I know I'm no good as an actress. I have no talent. Even you won't work with me, but I'm dying to be good so you'll find me f-f-fascinating."

He smoked his pipe quietly for a couple of minutes, with me huddled against his chest. He stroked my head like he strokes Remus'. I thought he might scratch behind my ears. All I could think of then was planting daffodils and hyacinths. Finally, as I subsided, Bing spoke.

"Barry Gargon sent me word about a new TV film of *Our Town.*"

"You'll play the Stage Manager—correct?"

"Yes." Then he continued slyly, "And they think you might be right for Emily. Happy anniversary!"

CHAPTER 7

How To Keep Up with Bing

Long before our marriage, I knew that Bing, as they used to say in Edwardian days, was a man's man. Instead of an engagement ring, he had given me a saddle; right after we were wed, he gifted me with a 20-gauge Berretta and took me to Rising River Ranch where a hunting guide "just happened" to drop in.

I had crawled on hands and knees after Buzz Fiorini from the duck blind right into the middle of the flooded field. I had clinched chattering teeth together, peered into the imminent nightfall and, when Buzz shouted "Now!" into my hypersensitive ear, fired with fright at I knew not what. Bing waded straight out in front of me, beaming as he picked up a deceased teal from the water.

"Hey, congratulations! That was a great shot. You've got to be the Annie Oakley of the Brazos bottoms! Isn't that something, Buzz? She's going to be all right, don't you think? I might have to take her hunting with me all the time."

The die was cast. I was unalterably committed. Now I had to learn to shoot and fish on one hand, and keep him from ever finding out that I was the greatest fraud in field or by stream.

I tried to assume that Diana's prowess was inherited from my Dad, but the assumption was rash. Still, with Bing's tolerance, I have found that keenness and zest compensate for lack of ability.

Of course this doesn't work with all sports—like golf. Here I've had to be content in the role of sort of a chauffeur-spectator.

Oh, right after we married, while wallowing about in a quest for "togetherness," I took a few lessons. It was a frustrating experience! I really believe the golf swing is the most unnatural motion in all sports. I was so inept, so maladroit, that the possibility of my ever mastering it seemed beyond reach.

But I plugged determinedly on. I had blisters on my blisters, which, blessedly, turned into calluses. I was never allowed on the course. To my appeals, the pro merely grunted, "Nah, you might get hurt!"

"But," I wailed, "I hit that last one at least twenty-five yards!"

"Yes, you're getting more length, but also more width, and two out of three are air shots."

The fruitlessness of my travail became abundantly evident one day when I asked the pro if he thought that, after two more years of work, I'd be good enough for Bing to let me play with him in the mixed foursomes. "You mean the mixed gruesomes," he said pointedly. "I really couldn't say. You see, I'm single, and I've never been forced to play with a woman."

That did it! I saw that optimism was the refuge of the ignorant, and my four little Ben Hogan clubs, with my name on the clubheads, have long been gathering dust in the attic while I have become an ardent member of the gallery privileged to stand in back of the par three sixteenth tee at Cypress Point and advise the struggling professionals to "go for it," which means hitting a 220-yard shot into the teeth of the gale, over the raging sea to the distant green. And when their ball plops into the ocean, I smile smugly while they reach for another. I was there when Porky Oliver carded a 19 on the hole. No, as a golfer I was a vicarious participant.

Racing? I love horses. Hadn't I read *Black Beauty* and *Smokey, the Cowhorse* six times, weeping copiously over his plight? I had read Steinbeck's "Red Pony" and loved it. But thoroughbred racing was something else again. Bing's deep knowledge of lineage, "out-crosses," and the "bottom line"; his familiarity with the jargon of the track—weights, distances, and course conditions—was beyond my ken, and when he talked with elaborate pragmatism of "the form," he lost me.

It was like taking a crash course in Basque at Berlitz, but I was in the stands at The Curragh, holding a two-bob ticket in my hot little hand, when Meadow Court, the Irish three-year-old he owned with Canadians Max Bell and Frank McMahon, romped home in the Irish Derby. Shure, and it was a great day when Bing went out to the steward's stand to accept the cup. A great crowd surged around calling for a song, and Bing obliged with an *a cappella* rendition of "When Irish Eyes Are Smiling."

He was several times interrupted by a little Irishman, deep in the crowd, crying, "Bing, man, I can't see you!" Bing finally stopped and called out, "What do you want me to do?" The diminutive Gael replied quickly, "Would you iver stand on your wallet?"

Bing always averred that Meadow Court was a great horse, but all I really knew was that he had a soft muzzle and lovely brown eyes, and I was fond of the handsome cup which came to grace our regency table in the front hall.

My record in fishing—dry-fly fishing—is about as bad. Rising River Ranch, a tiny working spread where Leonard raises quarter horses and a few head of Angus, has been the scene of thousands of fruitless casts with Goofer Bugs, Blue Uprights and Black Gnats.

When Bing and I opened the season one early May, he let me use a spinning rig, with monotonous results: three casts, three fat browns or rainbows. Sometimes I caught a bird nest on a back cast, or a snag in the water, but the hungry fish went for the hardware with gusto. The only problem with this system was that once the three-fish limit was caught, I was out of action for the rest of the morning; so I'd lie quietly on the old wooden bridge, watching the fish feed below, or observe, out of the corner of the eye, the doe and her fawns in the shadows at the edge of the trees.

Bing, meanwhile, would be stalking the big ones that lurked under the stream's bank with a Black Gnat, or perhaps a Ginger Quill. He would crawl to the edge of the river, using a swatch of tules for cover, and let out his line in what seemed to be slow motion; one—two—three—forward—up, pause; forward—up—tip-

to-eleven-o'clock, pause. More and more line would glide rhyth-
mically through the air until—*flick!* The dry fly would settle in the
water some fifty feet away, just upstream of the dimpling trout.
As the fly drifted past its fish, Bing would give a short, sharp tug on
the line, then release again. Why? The fly was simulating difficulty,
unable to dry its wings, which should be more appealing to the
rainbow.

He didn't mention whether the illness was respiratory (as in an
air-breathing bug) or gastrointestinal (a touch of DDT), and
didn't seem amused when I put this query to him. "No talk on
the river!" he shushed imperatively, just as the 4½-pound trout
rose to the limping Ginger Quill. A battle royal ensued, with the
fish lunging for its hiding place in a muskrat hole under the bank,
and Bing trying to keep his rod tip up without breaking the leader.
Lots of talk *then*—even shouting.

I cheered him on, my man, cannily leading the recalcitrant fish
to his waiter's net with the frying pan to follow. His fierce concentration made victory inevitable. The rainbow leaped, shimmering in the sun; he dived, tearing off line so fast the reel hummed;
he raced downriver, leaving a wake of white bubbles *v*-ing out
behind; he sulked near the reeds, then made sudden lunges for the
muskrat holes. If he ever made one, it would have spelled disaster.

Bing laughed, he sang, he coaxed, he crooned, he cursed as his
pipe fell into the stream—to be retrieved by Remus—and gently,
deftly, he guided the sleek monster finally into the net.

"What a catch, darling! What a catch!" My heart was still in
my throat. I'd been running up and down the bank, falling into
fresh cow dabs, tripping over roots, trying to wash some of the
mud from Bing's pipe, and shooing away the gallery of interested
heifers.

"Well, if you get tired of being a market fisherman and put up
that spinning rig, I'll show you how to get some action like this."

So I did, and he did. At least he tried. He stood for hours saying
"One-two-three" to synchronize our casting arms. He attached a
shooting line to my leader and from the bridge I could achieve real
distance, but I had a tendency to drop my rod tip at the top of my
back cast, and after I had inextricably engaged my seventh blue

upright in the weeping willows, he regarded me with understandable exasperation. "Honey," he said gently, if unelegantly, "you handle that thing like a cow with a musket. I tell you what, I'll catch 'em and you cook 'em. You've got a good stroke with a skillet."

Last year, while he was wet-fly fishing for salmon on the River Derwent in Cockermouth, England, he only let me join him for lunch, explaining, "They're dour, dear, since the river's in spate. You wouldn't enjoy casting here."

And off he went with the Gilly, Joe Brooks, and a camera crew for the *American Sportsman*. All eyes were shining, all appetites were whetted for the fish stories to come. So I contented myself with riding down the twisting lanes to the Trout Inn, where I dreamed of the ones that were getting away.

But Bing still has faith. He always wanted a "buddy," not a sweetheart, so we two share the excitement, the stories, the frustrations that accompany a hunting trip. We've been after birds in many places, but a trip I remember vividly was one we made with Trader Vic and Helen Bergeron to Lawrence and Leonora Woods' ranch near Refugio, Texas.

For a split second he just stood there, Jake did, frozen in the instinctive realization that right in front of his nose was a—or maybe several—bobwhite quail. His tail was pointed out and up like a semaphore, the right foreleg lifted in signal, almost waving us to come on: *Hurry up—I have 'em here!*

I was just a few steps behind, and was almost ready when the explosion occurred. One—two—three—four balls of fluff came zooming out from in front of the dog, who never moved. I swung and fired. *Wham!* Not one, but two shells went off in my brand-new little 28-Accirio Speciale Boehler. The quail kept whirring on their merry way, and I glanced apologetically at Frank, our guide.

Frank's look could have frozen Lot and his whole family, and he bit off his words like he was eating jerky. "I told you it'd double-fire, and not to put but one shell in that gun."

"I'm sorry, Frank." There wasn't much else to say, not when he looked like that.

Then, when one of the dogs ranged too far and Frank called him back with colorful invective imputing illegitimacy and ineptitude, I hoped to inject a note of humor. "I must be just as stupid as the dogs this morning."

Frank turned quickly and proudly. "We don't have no stupid dogs around here, Mrs. Crosby." He said it with such a telling emphasis on "dogs" that I knew who was the stupid one.

Very shortly we were coming up onto a slough. The mesquite was dripping from last night's downpour, and our shiny black "Santa Claus boots" were proving very useful. In fact, the water was halfway up to our knees. I didn't care. I didn't care if I fell down and drowned. I wasn't shooting any quail, while Helen Bergeron and our hostess, Leonora Woods, practically had their limits.

Frank Osborne, who handled the dogs and found the quail, was about to lose his perfect record. He'd already lost his temper. We sloshed away. Well, I might not be able to shoot, but I could keep up with him, even though he was used to walking twenty miles a day.

After about five minutes of utter silence, Frank said, "You know, Mrs. Crosby, you're not like a lot of those out-of-state visitors. You're kind of a different breed of heifer. You come from anywhere around here?"

Well, the sun was shining again. "Yes, Frank. I went to school not a hundred miles from here—Robstown, Texas, near Corpus Christi."

"Better sit down a minute and rest the dogs." So we sat on the one dry spot in the area. I broke my gun for safety and then thought: It's so good to be back in this country. Though I'd never been on a ranch like the Woods's ranch, growing cattle and oil wells indiscriminately, I'd known lots of people like the Woodses—warm and friendly and open, and distinctly Texan, and I sure had loved growing up in the valley—the golden valley with its three crops a year, mesquite trees with thorns, prickly-pear cactus that bore the purple fruit every year, and the search for a cool breeze, like the one coming up now.

"Okay," said Frank, "let's get on with it." And we strode off again.

Pretty soon little Jacques, Frank's young spaniel, started wagging his tail like mad. "Somethin's there," said Frank. "Somethin's there. That's a good baby." The well-trained English pointers gave Jacques and his quarry a wide berth rather than honoring him, and I saw why. Two big jack rabbits flushed and Jacques tore out after them. "Well, I told you game was here," said Frank. Then he hollered a couple of ringing imprecations, and Jacques came back, still wagging.

A few seconds later Jacques came on proper point. Frank counseled, "Now walk up there slowly, Mrs. Crosby. Don't get in a hurry. There's lots of time. You just think they're going to blow up in your face. When they get up, you swing up free and keep that barrel moving. Then you pull that trigger. Just squeeze a little bit."

It was as if he had written it in a book. The bird flushed. I swung the gun up to my shoulders, never taking my eye off the bird, squeezed the trigger, and the bird dropped. There was only one shell in the gun this time—no chance of a double fire.

"That's what I mean now. You'll get 'em. It won't take forever."

As I proudly marched on, I thought of the first time Daddy took me hunting in Texas—to Mr. Hobbins' lease. Mr. Fred and Dad had been friends for many years, and his home was just a few miles out in the country from West Columbia. Mrs. Hobbins greeted us on this particular morning with fried sausage, biscuits, and homemade plum preserves—just to tide us over until lunchtime.

Then Daddy took me out in the palmetto thickets, which were like a jungle. Big pecan trees, like those we had around the house in West Columbia, oak trees hung with thick grapevines, and Spanish moss dripping from the trunks. Dad knew his way perfectly. The area was like Main Street in West Columbia to him, but not to me. I'd have been lost in a minute.

Then Daddy started teaching me the little tricks. Moss grows on the north side of the tree. A compass works thus and so. "Daddy, I believe that compass, and I'm delighted that you believe

I could use one, but I'll just sit here where you put me until you come back."

Dad laughed. "That might be the best thing you could do after all, pumpkin. I'll pick you up in an hour or so." And he disappeared silently into the jungle.

There I learned the secret of why so many men go hunting. It's quiet in the woods. When you're waiting for an animal to pass, there's so much time to think. The problems of today's living dissolve, just as Daddy dissolved into the woods.

He came back in an hour or two, having got his buck, but I'd got a lot more than that. I'd watched some deer play down by the Brazos River. I'd heard the mockingbird's song, and seen the saucy bluejay angry at a squirrel for stealing lunch, and the squirrel barking right back at him, flicking his bushy tail.

Yes, that had been my first hunt.

"Well, now, Mrs. Crosby, we better get to the wagon. Mr. Woods said we should meet him 'bout now, and we can do it 'cause you're not skunked no more." And he gave me a quick grin. "I thought for a little bit we'd have to get lost all day."

The wagon was a fantastic apparatus with gun holsters and racks, front fender seats for dogs or guide, a bar in the back with soft drinks, and rain gear, lap robes, sunglasses, and extra shells. The tires could handle monsoon or desert sand. There, sipping iced tea, were Lawrence, Bing, Trader Vic, Helen, and Leonora.

"We heard lots of shootin'. Any luck?" asked Lawrence.

Frank looked chagrined, but I gloated, "Of course! With Mr. Osborne breaking trail, I couldn't miss—once."

"Okay, then, let's change up sides. Leonora, you and Frank take Vic and Helen up toward that clump of trees; Kathryn, you and Bing follow me. We'll meet you all for lunch. Now, hit the brush!" So we marched off into the woods again. This time Lawrence was leading the way and handling the dogs.

There wasn't much chance of our bothering each other—there was plenty of room on this spread, plenty of room. It was about the biggest expanse of land I'd ever seen, except maybe for Bing's Elko ranch up in Nevada.

That was different, though: high mountains, snow five months a year. The one time we went there after Bing and I married, John Eacret and his men were riding the ranges day and night to get newborn calves on their feet and to milk before they froze in the wet April snow. Poisoned meat was put out for predators and scavengers who would pick the eyes from the newborn, or work a sore on the back of a cow until a fatal infection would set in. It was hard work, punishing work.

But Bing and John had a reason for their work. Bing's sons would inherit not only one of the finest ranches in Nevada, but would acquire values to be learned working there each summer with the regular hands: fixing fence, irrigating, digging ditches, working and moving cattle. A long list of chores, not all of them pleasant or colorful—like dehorning and branding, driving the buck rake, and pitching hay to hungry cows.

John Eacret had been a rodeo star who doubled Bing in some of his earlier pictures. He was a quiet, kind, no-nonsense man, who was straw boss over Bing's sons when most of their friends were at summer camp. Doris, John's wife, showed them how great girls can be. Doris could hunt and fish with the best of the men, and she kept books, had a garden, canned the produce of that, and flew her own plane. Her big brown eyes and wide smile kindled enthusiasm for each new project; offered comfort for each disappointment.

Bing wanted the ranch for his boys. Phillip and Dennis, the twins, had the most ranching ability. Gary had always wanted show business. Lindsay was still in school, and seemed to be a city boy. But Dennis had a way with animals.

John and Doris told me that he could walk up to any green horse in the early part of spring before he'd been ridden, slide on it bareback, and gentle it all the way to the corrals from the mountain ranges. Denny was a boy who could break all the broncs. But he didn't do it the swear and sweat way—the animals just seemed to know that here was a boy who could handle them.

Denny could heal animals too. He was a very good vet, though he hadn't studied it at Washington State. They told me that, when he was in Bellarmine High School, he concentrated harder on fighting on the football field than on anything else. It was hard to believe with that gentle nature now. He had been All Northern California halfback one year.

While Phillip didn't have Denny's knack for animals, he always had a charming personality with people and was a very hard worker, so together they should have been a great team at Elko.

But one sad day the boys, who were now young men, talked with their Dad and averred that ranch life was too tough for them. They also wanted show business.

"That's pretty tough, too," said Bing.

But they wanted to try, so the ranch was sold. Bing never went back.

"Heads up," shouted Bing. "Jake on point."

"Just take it easy, Kathryn," said Lawrence. "Sneak up here to the left. Walk up right behind the dog and, if you're lucky, the quail will flush going away and you can raise your gun and get him."

I eased forward. The bomb burst. Three birds were out. I shot and missed them all. Bing picked off one and Lawrence the other, and they looked at me and laughed.

"All right, Annie Oakley. You really don't have to shoot from the hip."

"Didn't I give them enough time?"

"Honey, it's a good thing that you didn't hit the bird. It would have steak tartare. Let him get out a ways—you'll have a bigger pattern. Don't get excited."

"I was born that way."

"A little patience, my dear."

"Sure—patience. You just wait until little Ole Roberto Blanco busts out. I'll patience him."

"Why do you only have one shell in your gun?"

"Oh, a little pact I made with Frank this morning, honey. I put one shell in my gun because if I put two shells in, I pull the trigger twice before I think about it, and the whole thing sounds like a time bomb going off."

"Mmmmmm—well, if it's all right with you, walk ahead of me, would you, dear?"

"Yes, Kathryn." Lawrence twinkled. "I think you might do well ahead of both of us, then Bing and I can stay back here and direct the activities."

"Don't worry, fellas. I haven't shot a man yet."

"That's a good record, Kathryn," praised our host. "I think I'd like to keep it that way. Besides, we ought to be getting back for lunch soon. I have to run into Refugio this afternoon and check into the political situation. There's an election today, and I'm running for the Board of Supervisors. I stand a good chance of getting whipped, and I don't want the people to think I skulked out of town just on that account."

"You mean you're up for election today, and you're out here hunting quail? Why, you should have told us. We'd all be down at the courthouse passing out cards for you."

"How did you know about passing out cards?"

"Oh, Lawrence, I've done that all my life. Dad was County Commissioner for five two-year terms in Brazoria County."

"He must be quite a man."

"The best! He was on the Court of the fifth-richest county in Texas. They were assessed for $62,000,000. He helped to equalize values and, as a result, the assessed value is now $288,000,-000. After he lost out a few years back, he taught school until his retirement just a couple of years ago. Now he's doing what you're doing now. He's hunting and fishing, and having a wonderful time."

Then inspiration hit me. "Listen! Why don't we go down to the polls right now? Maybe Bing could sing a few songs—draw a crowd, and you could give them your message."

"Time, darling, time. I'm not politically inclined, and you know it. I eschew anything controversial or political."

Suddenly right under our feet a covey rose and flew straight away. I could ignore all mathematical equations about "lead" and "swing." I poked and got me a quail, then reloaded and got me another that was nearly out of range. A double the hard way!

Bing accepted Lawrence's accolades in my behalf and gloated, "She's just penciled in now, but a few more shots like that and I'll have to ink her in permanently."

We were slogging down a little ravine now, full of oak trees. "Lunch is pretty soon," said Lawrence. "I think we better get on to the big oaks."

We continued on to join the others. And I gasped. Leonora had accomplished a miracle in a cluster of gnarled trees. A powder room had been set up with mirrors, cologne, and linen towels. There were some wind chimes hanging from a branch and tinkling in the breeze. The campfire was going, and the hammock strung up between the trees was especially inviting. Stained-glass birds perched in the oaks' lower limbs, reflecting the sun's rays, and the muted music of the mockingbirds underscored the idyllic scene.

Trader Vic was showing Chuy how to give the frijoles the Señor Pico treatment (Chuy's interest was somewhat detached). Vic and Bing broke into "That's where my money goes . . ." in rather tentative harmony, but when Lawrence added his competent baritone, some quite good barbershop ensued. Helen, Leonora, and I visited, as Texas women are wont to do, and it wasn't long before I succumbed to the hammock's invitation.

I had my eyes half closed, almost pretending to be asleep, and I heard Bing regaling the group with the story of Phil Harris' last duck shoot at Rising River.

"Now, young Bill, Frances' and Leonard's boy, is a red-haired freckle-faced refugee from Tom Sawyer's gang. By the time he was twelve, he was probably the most insatiable duck hunter of our time—juvenile or adult, and a good shot. Of course the opportunity to shoot with his idol, Phil (or Uncle Phil Harris, as he calls him) just adds icing to the cake, and when Phil came up for a visit to the ranch last fall and promised to take him out on a Saturday morning at six, he was in hog heaven.

"Frances, Kathryn's sister, was in Redding doing a style show, so Phil and Leonard, being all alone, drove into Burney to bowl. They quaffed a few, and it was five A.M. before the two celebrants, weary and heavy-lidded for want of sleep, drove back to the ranch.

" 'Phil, old buddy, you're going to have to sleep mighty fast.'

" 'Why is that?' muttered Phil through the bourbon.

" 'Because you made a date to shoot ducks with Billy at six o'clock this morning,' replied Leonard.

" 'Oh, well,' Phil said, 'he's probably forgotten all about it, and besides that, he'll never get up at six o'clock.'

" 'He gets up at six o'clock to go to school,' was Leonard's retort.

" 'My lord, Abe Lincoln never got up that early.'

" 'Well, Bill does!'

"Phil ruminated for a moment. 'Tell you what we do,' he said. 'We'll shut off the engine at the front gate, sneak up the stairs, and into the house, and he'll never know the difference.'

"Len was unconvinced, but that's what they did. They tiptoed up the step, across the porch, and just as they reached the door, it burst open and there stood Billy in wader's jacket and cap, gun in hand, his Lab, Porgy, at his side, and his duck call in his mouth calling stridently, *quack, quack, quack,* like a whole flock of mallards.

"There was nothing Phil could do but pump himself up with three or four cups of black coffee, and a couple of No-Doze tablets, and away they went.

"Bill got his limit and Phil's too—but then the Indian was hardly himself!"

The hunters chuckled.

How lucky I was to be included on a trip like this. This was strictly men's province, and I knew it well, but we three girls were included. I remembered Trader Vic saying in his typical Wally Beery delivery, "Shucks, I wouldn't go shootin' without Helen. It wouldn't be any fun—and what's the point? To see who can tell the biggest lies and swallow the most whiskey? Why, when I see my bride here make a good shot like that double she downed this morning by the creek bed—hot dog, that's worth the trip to Texas."

"Now, Victor dear," Helen murmured softly.

"No, gol-darn it, I mean it. . . ."

"Well, dear, I've been shooting with you quite a few years now. I should be able to hit one or two."

Why couldn't I be modest like that? Why couldn't I shoot like that?

Luxuriating in these happy thoughts, I was just dozing off when I heard Bing cry, "And there she is—Miss Fat Stock of 1950."

Instantly awake, I tried to sit up and fell out of the hammock. "I was not Miss Fat Stock. I was the Queen of the Houston Rodeo and Fat Stock Exposition. It was my classmates that started that other terrible title, and you who perpetuated it," I said, all the while fighting my way out of the bushes and dead oak leaves as Leonora and Helen joined the men in their laughter.

"Anyhow, I was thinking about Vic's argument for lady hunters, and I'm for that! Now what about lady salmon fishermen. I know we'd look better than you do in the long flannel nighties George brought you to wear."

Bing grinned and explained to the others, George Rosenberg, his agent, went with them last year for some salmon out of the Strait of Juan de Fuca. Canadian Capers they called that trip.

Bill Morrow, the writer, was there, and Phil Harris, and Dick Snideman, a Chicago businessman, Ed Crowley, Sheraton Hotel man, and Buster Collier from San Francisco. Max Bell, the Canadian who loaned them the yacht, didn't come along, but he should have. He'd have picked up a few stories for his newspapers.

Buster Collier is an avid sportsman, with the very latest in equipment, the latest attire from Abercrombie and Fitch, the latest boots by Gokey. His fishing impedimenta is vast. That day, as they were climbing into the outboard motorboats for the salmon trolling, Bill Morrow noted Buster had two small packages about as big as a box of kitchen matches. "What are those?" Bill asked.

"Well," said Buster patronizingly, "you chaps just don't keep abreast of the times. You clip one of these to your jacket, and if you fall overboard, pull this string and it inflates."

"How long will it hold you up?" asked Bill.

"Until you're hoarse," said Phil quickly.

Dick, being a complete neophyte with rod and reel, was selected as Phil's boatman, where he'd have a chance to watch an expert at work.

On the second day out, Phil hooked a thirty-eight-pound salmon on a fly rod. Whipping and boating was going to be a problem. They were about six miles offshore, and Dick, certainly no Gar Wood, was at the wheel of the sixteen-footer. While playing the fish with all his native skill, Phil was crying hoarsely to Dick, "Turn left . . . turn right . . . follow him . . . back . . . dammit—back . . . right, right, you idiot . . . right . . . faster . . . slower . . ."

Dick told us later what happened. He was trying desperately to comply with all those commands issued simultaneously, but the boat was spinning around in a tight circle. The inevitable happened: The salmon got under the boat, whereupon Phil swung on Dick and cried, "Now you've done it! Just for that get out of the boat. Out! Out!" He grabbed the wheel with his free hand, leaving Dick to stare out over the vast expanse of open ocean and wonder just where he would go.

Happily for Dick the salmon swam out from under the boat just about then, and Phil got busy. He got the fish, too.

There were more hunting and fishing stories, more barbershop harmony, and then the lunch was nearly ready: lamb barbecue, polenta (a kind of casserole out of grits), frijoles. I suddenly remembered I'd walked a few miles and was starved.

Leonora looked at Lawrence, then said softly, "Darlin', I hoped we'd be able to get some fresh seafood to start with, but I guess not."

Suddenly the sun was covered by the whirling blades of a helicopter. What in the world was a helicopter doing here? Leonora looked up. "Now isn't that the sweetest thing. That must be Dan."

The craft hovered a minute, then landed, and Mr. Landon got out carrying two quart mason jars. "Here, Leonora, I thought you'd want some Matagorda oysters for a starter. I picked them up an hour ago."

"Well, Dan, that's the nicest thing. They'll be delicious."

And the pilot followed him with a sackful of blue crabs. "Big blues—caught today. I bet Trader Vic has a good sauce up his sleeve."

"We'll have them right now. Come on and pull up a chair."

Bing pulled me aside and surreptitiously asked, "Y'all do this all the time down here?"

"Honey, you're in Texas. We don't mess around with box lunches here."

CHAPTER 8

How To Get Away from It All

The little Aero Commander was at the Burbank Airport when I drove over from Queen of Angels. I had left the floor (Post-Surgical Care in Orthopedics) at 11:00 A.M. sharp. If there were any delays, we wouldn't reach Las Cruces before nightfall—illegal and dangerous.

Rosemary Clooney was waiting—Rosie and Mary Frances and Nathaniel. Nathaniel had come to the field just to say good-bye to us tourists. We were seeking surcease and we didn't need any big fat babies to care for. Rosie's house was full of offspring—Miguel, María, Gabriel, Monsita, and Rafael—and she was stealing time to get some rest and be with Bing and me in our hideaway below the border. Of course those two were going to tape a few radio shows just so the trip wouldn't be a total loss, but this was a rest time, a quiet time.

Then Nathaniel cooed, and with one look of total understanding, Rosie spoke for me. "Let's take him."

Bridget gasped, then said, "But there's nothing for the wee pet to wear."

"It's warm down there. Come on, love. Come on, sister, and Kathryn." And we clambered aboard with the picnic lunch.

Mary Frances was copilot, and I held Nathaniel during takeoff. He was a real space-age baby—serene during noise, speed, air turbulence. As we rose, bouncing just enough to make me green, Mary Frances squealed, "Oh, Mom, the plane is dancing!"

Once above the clouds, the miles floated by. Rosie seemed to be napping. Her pale skin was translucent, her nose tip tilted, just enough to make me realize that she and Bing should be sister and brother as well as friends. No wonder they had worked for fifteen years with never a complication, singing in effortless harmony and exchanging rapid repartee with esprit and timing which revealed kindred feelings. No, *simpático* was the correct word for their relationship—*muy simpático.*

Thus, when Bing was surgically incapacitated, Rosie would appear from nowhere to share my vigil; when Halloween brought a bob-for-apples party, her gremlins joined our witches for tag on the lawn and fried chicken legs. Just a week ago, Bing had broken into my research of the renal portal system to say:

"You know, Rosie and I need to tape a few radio shows to finish off the season. We could do them here, or"—with a grin— "we could do them in Las Cruces. Rosie has been going full out lately. I'm a little worried about her—with those kids and the tours. What do you think? She's never seen that part of the country. It might be a nice change."

"Fantástico, querido."

I called our friend. She said, *"Sí."* And now we were beginning the luxurious process of unwinding. I stretched a bit, and Nathaniel retaliated with a foot to the ribs. His eyelashes fluttered a little, then he lay still. Mary Frances was just a lump in the corner now. Amazing that so much energy could totally subside in a second.

At San Diego we were down and up again in a matter of minutes, and clearing customs at Tijuana was accomplished with dispatch, and a modicum of red tape. Even now Rosie's eyes were sparkling and her color heightening. Yes, this was going to be good for her. I was so pleased that Bing worried about her. When I even tried to complain of fatigue, frustration, fear, he'd snort, "You're strong as a bull." But Rosie was different—delicate, delightful. Yes, we'd take care of her.

Hmmmmm—as if I thought I could really care for anyone. Why, this was the same airport where I had once feared I would end my days—in Tijuana (it means "Aunt Jane"). As the pilot refueled and we all sipped Coca Cola, I told Mary Frances once more about Mommy's sticky adventure as a wetback.

"It was this way, Mary Frances. Mary Morrow and a Texas friend, Belle Lang, and I had been hatching a plot to drive to the west coast of Mexico to Mexico City. We called it our Tamale Safari. We had no reservations anywhere along the line because Mary said, 'There are only two ways to get rooms in Mexico. One way is to send a deposit six months in advance, knowing the manager beforehand. The second is to arrive bag and baggage in the lobby and look sad, forlorn, and lost.' We chose the latter course; first, because we didn't have the money to deposit anywhere; and second, because it was more fun.

"Since we were vagabonds, we had to watch our pesos carefully. We'd eat lightly at breakfast and lunch—a mango, a papaya, maybe a hard-boiled egg. Then, when we arrived at our destination and had looked wistful enough to get a fine suite, we'd go to the hotel dining room and have our one good meal for the day. Mary and I rationalized it was a safeguard against *turista*. Poor Belle yearned agonizingly for three square meals a day, but we were firm.

"In Guaymas we went fishing for sailfish. Mary and I got the fish, and Belle got seasick.

"In Mazatlán we became beachcombers, resting at noon in the hammocks under the little thatched sun shelters, and my nose peeled.

"In Mexico City we stayed in a strange place the first night. It was a conference room, I think; but the second day we were admitted to the Geneva Hotel. The perfect spot for three young unchaperoned girls.

"Daddy's friend, Bruno Pagliai, took us to the races, and to dinner at his home. Yes, sweetheart, that's where you and Harry went swimming and had lunch with Bruno and Francesca when Daddy last took us to Mexico City. But my adventure was so long ago. Mr. Pagliai hadn't met Merle Oberon, and my name was still Kathryn Grant.

"Now, on our drive back to the States, stopping for the night in Mazatlán, I received word that Columbia Pictures needed me for retakes on *Guns of Fort Petticoat*. Mary, Belle, and I dashed for the airport, but it was late at night and there was nothing there—nothing but frogs and crickets chirping, and a sleepy janitor leaning on his broom, a little amazed to see three *gringas* in his nice airport. He told us the *jefe* was not there.

"I turned to Mary desperately. 'Where could he be?' She was now the expert on Latin American affairs.

" 'Well, he could be at the movies, or he could be home having his dinner. He'll be back—either tonight or tomorrow,' she said.

"So we went back to the hotel and tried to get organized. We decided to leave all the suitcases in the back of Belle's car, but because I was going to see your daddy very shortly after I returned, I wanted to take my elephant-shaped *piñata*. Inside the *piñata* I packed a colorful Mexican shirt and my Rolleiflex camera.

"Bright and early the next morning we drove back to the airport. There were no seats on the plane that day. I stood at the counter batting my eyes and looking very downcast until a lawyer said, 'I think you can purchase *one*.' So I grandly pulled out my checkbook. The *jefe*, who had returned from the movie 'the next day,' said, 'We do not accept checks.' So the lawyer also cashed my check.

"We anxiously waited until the plane arrived from Mexico City and Guadalajara—and there was room for me!"

"Oh, goody!" squeaked Mary Frances, who had heard the saga sixty times.

"Carrying my small bundle, I boarded the plane. This had been an exciting trip. I didn't know how exciting it was yet to be.

"I slept all the way to the landing at Tijuana. Then I realized I hadn't brought my suitcase. I hadn't brought my tourist visa. I hadn't brought my vaccination certificate, and I hadn't brought my purse with money—M-O-N-E-Y.

"As we got off the plane for immigration, I looked around hopefully—acres of red clay with the hot sun beating down. What a hopeless place to be stranded! There I was—fat, dumb, and unhappy with my teeth in my dry mouth and that silly elephant *piñata* under my arm. I yearned to get inside him and, slowly suffocating, succumb."

"Poor Mommy," sympathized Mary Frances, her eyes huge and round.

"I looked at the Spanish inspector. He looked at me. Well, the time had come. *'Por favor, señor,* I am an American movie actress." His gaze never wavered. What movie actress would go around with no luggage, carrying an elephant under her left arm?

" 'Yes?' He smiled.

" 'And I must go back to Los Angeles. You see, we are shooting a movie, and I must be there for retakes.'

" 'Yes?'

"Obviously he had never heard of retakes. I stood there and tried to look stoic. Then I looked outside. There was that red clay . . . in every direction, as far as the eye could see—red clay.

"So I cried. Just like you're doing, sweetheart, but don't you remember what he said next? *'Vente! Vente!'* " ("Go! Go!")

"And you got back on the plane!" exulted my daughter, whose free flow tears stopped with this turn of the story.

"Exactly. And now Tijuana doesn't look scary at all, does it? But I wonder if *el inspector* is the same man who let me through before. What do you think?"

As we walked back to the plane, Mary Frances curtsied gravely to the man in uniform and murmured, *"Muchas gracias."*

Back aboard and airborne, we attacked the lunch: shrimp, ham-and-cheese-layer sandwiches, huge juicy peaches, milk and hot tea.

Rosie looked down at the seemingly barren terrain, then asked, "Kathryn, how in the world did you find this land? There aren't even roads down there, much less towns."

"There's a road somewhere—or was, before the last flash flood. But you're right, it's like discovering the end of the world. Bing found it on a fishing trip with Bill Morrow. He was looking for marlin and the quest took him to Mazatlán, Mexico, where he heard reports of a billfish concentration near the tip of Baja California. The two, following this lead, chartered a plane and landed at Las Cruces Palmilla, right at the end of the peninsula. Bing wrote me about the handsome hotel, the enchanting people, the dramatic environment, then slid in the offhand invitation, 'If you'll hurry up with that picture Mr. Preminger has you wandering around in, you can help me pick out a home site. I'd like to build further up in the Sea of Cortés [the Gulf of California] around Rancho Las Cruces.' "

"Just like that?"

"Just like that!"

We flew along, past Ensenada, almost to Rosario on the Pacific side. Then we crossed over the Sierra San Miguel to Santa María, the Bahía de los Angeles and were to follow the coast line all the way down, past Santa Rosalía, Mulegé, Loreto, with a stop at La Paz for customs. Then a zip over the mountains to Las Cruces.

"I had thought Bing would forget about the house; he had been so casual in his approach, but soon plans arrived—plans that he had evolved with the landowner, Rod Rodriguez. They were good too, though their execution gave me nightmares.

"Andres, the native *ingeniero,* scorned plans, transits, or plumb bobs, relying on his naked eye, a length of string, and a mystical native instinct. The walls of the house are a bit crooked here and there, and the sliding doors won't stay on the track, but the house has high ceilings, thick walls, and stone patios on all sides. There were some moments of near panic when Bing saw there was no framing for electricity, plumbing, or cabinets, but then the *trabajadores* simply took sledgehammers and crowbars and whacked out the necessary apertures."

"Did you have anything to do with the house?"

"Oh, sure, Rosie, I had *something* to do with the house. I almost wrecked it before we even got started. Because of my clever caper, I could have been in a Mexican hoosegow for up to thirty years if Bing hadn't rescued me."

"Was this the hot-check episode?"

"Exactly."

"Girl, you really pulled a beauty there! Bing was telling me about it at our last recording session."

"He tells everybody. But when Bing's sick, he crawls into his shell like an affronted armadillo. He doesn't like to bother me, so he just doesn't say anything, and I go into a swivet wondering what I've done to put him off. The last time he had a kidney-stone attack, he didn't want me around at all.

"Before the surgery, to keep from thinking about the knife that was poised, we talked about the house at Las Cruces, and how it was coming, and how after he was better, I'd go down and see to things. The moment he became conscious post-operatively, he said, 'All right, get packed and go.'

". . . remember, when I told you to study up on the Latin temperament when you married Joe because you married a Latin, and then you retorted just as quickly, 'Don't forget he's marrying an Irish girl'? Well, Bing married a girl who is accustomed to hovering when those she loves are sick. The Grandstaffs come from a long line of hoverers—and all the branches, the Stokelys, the Sullivans—we're all very good hoverers. And there he was, right out of anesthesia, saying, 'Go away from me. I don't want you.' Not in so many words, but clearly that was the idea.

"I called Mary Morrow and she must have appreciated the urgency. I said, 'We're going to Mexico tomorrow.' And she said, 'Okay, honey, I'll be ready.'

"Mary and I flew down here and became involved in elaborate consultations with the carpenter, Salvador Castelano, who finally got the idea that when I said *ventana de rosa,* a rose window, what I really meant was an ox-eye window, *ojo de buey.*"

"Why would it be called ox-eye?"

"Well, the ox squints like that, and his pupils go double, and that's the end result."

"How you lika dat!"

"We went to La Paz and, on Bing's instructions, I transferred twenty-five thousand pesos from his account to a checking account of my own. Then I began the assigned task of furnishing Casa Crosby. In La Paz I bought a *congelador* (freezer), *horno* (an oven), *friadoro,* and *estufa* de las *quemedores.* Also a *lavadora automática* (a washing machine)."

"*Cosas para la cocina* (things for the kitchen)?"

"*Muy bien.* Joe's been tutoring you. I should have had you with me instead of that dictionary. Then Mary and I went to Mexico City. I really lost my head there! We found at Ramon Aranda the beautiful Mexican screen that became the headboard in our bedroom; hardware at Penuoles Xiga.

"At the National Pawn Shop (Mountain of Pity), we found a red-and-green chest with mirror diamonds inset on the sides. By that time we'd finished the nursery—and my checkbook.

"But that didn't stop me. I picked up a blank checkbook and wrote blithely on. One day we went to La Granja, owned by Señor Paco Gonzales, a soft-spoken Castillian. He showed us acres of lovely furniture, but all the time he was looking at Mary and breathing '*Preciosa, hermosa*' in his soft, lisping Spanish. I thought he might be talking about the furniture, but his eyes never left Mary.

"We bought a few nice things, including a fine old Elizabethan sideboard, and then, leaving shipping instructions for the heavy things with the various merchants, we carried whatever the plane would hold out to the airport—things like the white enamel toilet and the bidet, which our pilot carried, happily ignorant of its function. He thought it was a bird bath.

"We stopped for lunch in Taxco and visited the shop of William Spratling, a *gringo* who has lived there for thirty years and works in sterling. We purchased a tiny fish made of silver that was jointed and would wiggle on the table, some flatware, and we were off to Las Cruces.

"Imagine my chagrin when Mr. Spratling's letter arrived a few weeks later. It said something like,

Dear Kathryn,
After our pleasant little visit the other day, I just hate to tell you that the check you wrote me was a bit of a bouncer. But don't worry about it, honey, if you're in the shorts right now, just accept that little fish as a gift from me. Send cash for the flatware.

Sincerely,
Bill Spratling

"That was the tip-off. From then on the hot checks started rolling in. Bing, who was up and around, nearly flattened me. I had transferred pesos and spent dollars. It took him six months to get us out of hock. After that we traveled as 'Bing Crosby and wife,' trying not to be too specific about my name."

We checked in and out of La Paz and immediately after take-off, I cautioned Rosie to get ready for the landing. The pilot took us in the back door. We circled a mountain, a small one, and then started wending our way through a deep canyon, with precipitous cliffs on either side—seemingly close enough to touch.

Rosie and I could see the burros on the side of the hill. The land that looked devoid of growth from the air was covered with cacti. We could even see the wild figs growing, clinging to rocks, showing as much below the ground level as above, the gray roots exposed while they struggled into the rock for any bit of nourishment that might be gleaned.

We were being buffeted around by down drafts, but mercifully we made a smooth landing on the very short strip. I jigglingly explained that it was much safer to land up the slot this way because if there was any emergency we could go up again over the ocean. Coming in off the sea, if anything went wrong, there'd be no place to go—just mountains.

Mary Frances tumbled out, to be followed by me with Nathaniel in my arms.

"Hey, where did you get the stowaway?" cried Bing with a great show of surprise. He took the grinning, happy cherub from me just in time for me to break up a footrace between the older two down the runway while Roger Bacon's Apache was on its final leg.

About this time Rosie emerged, white-faced and shaking a bit. "What goes, Rose?" asked Bing. "That hairy approach shake you?"

"Listen," said Rosie, "Lindbergh got three days of confetti for less than that!"

"Nah—that's a standard approach, and besides, it's good for the bar business. Now hop in the beach buggy and we'll run up to Casa Crosby. Chavalo will bring your bags."

Everybody piled in and we bounced along over the rutted, rocky road through the tall palm trees girding the beach. There were six boats at the muey—all flying marlin flags.

"Ah, you got fish today."

Then Harry shrieked from the back seat, "Daddy got two, and I almost got one."

"What about fishing tomorrow, Rosie?" asked Bing. "I think you'll like it the way we do it here."

"I'm pretty apt to get seasick, Bing."

"No, not here. There's too much excitement. We fish with *voladores*—flying fish—suspended from outriggers, and a strike is just the equivalent of dynamite."

Harry cut in. "Oh, Aunt Rosie. You'll get to hear Nino—he's the boat captain—scream *marlín, marlín, marlín*. I can speak Spanish, did you know that? Then if you catch him, you get to put up this flag with a picture of a marlin on it, and Daddy always turns them loose, but he puts a tag in their back, and the tag is . . . what's the tag, Daddy?"

"It's part of the Woods Hole Conservation project. We don't bring in the fish here."

"Never?"

"The first time the fishermen catch one for picture and congratulations, and then, unless it's a record, we tag them and release them. The fish dissolves that hook in three days. He's not hurt, and he'll live to give someone else some great sport. The Woods Hole people are trying to trace the migratory patterns of the fish, find their breeding grounds. If the fish is caught again, and the tag is found, he sends it in, tells where he caught it, and gets a dollar."

We pulled past the *prado* and stopped by the stucco house with the red tile roof.

"Got to paint those tiles white. Reflects the heat, they tell me," said Bing.

Rosie took a long look, taking in the curving arches, the bubbling fountain, and the stone patio cooled by Indian laurels, and dotted here and there by plantings of marailla.

"You kids are tucked away pretty good here."

We strolled through cool arches to *la sala de huéspedes* (guest room). Harry, heavily smitten by Rosemary's blond beauty, opened the sliding screen door with such élan that it slipped off the track and hit the tile floor with a great crash! The *orioncitos* in the porch lamp fluttered out in fright, and Rosie laughed—a lovely, throaty laugh.

Bing struggled with the door. "Aren't you glad we could get you away from all those children? All right—suit up, everybody. We have time for a swim before supper."

Rosie's tiny room looked like a bridal bower, the hanging cross and candelabra draped with cascades of fuchsia bougainvillaea. Tangerine hibiscus filled the vases; plumeria's heavy scent evoked a deep sigh.

"Do you think the *mariaches* need a girl singer? I can handle 'Besame Mucho.' "

She peered out the stucco rose window in her shower. "So I can always see Las Cruces?"

"Yes, and you're the only one guaranteed to have hot water."

Minutes later we were wending our way down the hill to the *playa*. We passed the elephant trees cautiously, their papery bark was reputed to burn the skin. The *palo blanco* rustled in the breeze, the flame trees glowed scarlet. The tide was out, the water absolutely flat, so the fishing boats were mirrored perfectly.

Rosie and Harry became snorkling buddies. Mary Frances joined hands with me, and we all hit the soft warm water. Only Nathaniel stayed ashore, crawling after a Sally Lightfoot while Enriqueta, our *niñera,* saw to it that the crab eluded him.

Through the masks, the world of angelfish became ours. Angelfish and parrot fish, needlefish, and yellow and black sergeants major. Bing swam out to the True Love's mooring and then shouted.

"I can get your house on the ship-to-shore radio. Any message for your mother or Joe?"

"Tell them I'm fine and might never come home!"

I knew the feeling. Every time I saw a sunset like this, I ached —grim realization that Monday morning's alarm would prod me back into action at the hospital; and Rosie had a tour of Japan and Australia ahead of her. But now Nathaniel was crying, so we four snorklers swam for shore.

We came over the smooth round rocks to hear Harry, with all the wisdom of his four years. "Ah, it's nuthin', Aunt Rosie, he's just yellin' because he can't catch an isopod. Here, Nathaniel, I'll get you one." And with a lightning snatch, Harry caught two dock lice and presented them to his brother.

"Won't he eat those things, Harry?" queried Rosie.

"No, ma'am. He just lets them crawl around, then lets them go. Hey! I'll show you something!" Then Harry flipped over a rock and exposed a mass of brittle stars, some rockworms, and purple sea anemones.

Soon Rosie was scouring the beach and flipping over rocks like a field worker in a marine biology class. She learned to sneak up on chitons and lift them before their suction glued them too tightly. Mary Frances brought handfuls of hermit crabs in tiny shells to show Nathaniel and then came up with a sea cucumber.

"Look, Aunt Rosie. This is a sea cabbage. You must be careful when you handle it or . . ." And she looked very guilty as the poor creature eviscerated itself, oozing slimily onto the rocks and leaving Mary Frances holding the skin.

Just then Juan Geraldo Sanchez appeared. *"Buenos tardes,* Sra. Crosby," he said. He spoke carefully, clearly, as he shook hands and bowed formally. His huge, well-spaced brown eyes, firm chin, and proud mien seemed to promise that he would be a handsome young man when he grew up. Now, at twelve years old, he had an insatiable need for food and education.

I introduced him to Rosie, who graciously acknowledged his sweeping bow. A moment's silence ensued as Juan gazed seaward, looking for all the world like a conquistador of old. Rosie wanted to know what he did at Las Cruces, and Juan told her with great pride, and with me interpreting, that he was assistant gardener at Casa Crosby. But most importantly, he said, with eyes shining, he was a student.

Poor angel. I think he is a genius. What can the future hold for Juan? I first met him after I began teaching the ABC's to Victor and Antonio, Enriqueta's older boys. We had gathered for a session at our house where, on the patio, fountain tinkling in the background, I instructed in *los números* and *las letras*. Next day, being warm, I put our three and Enriqueta's two in the beach buggy. We would practice writing with sticks in the sand, and take a swim at recess time.

Halfway down the hill, this boy had appeared on the road. He waved, and we stopped the car. *"Es Juan, mi amigo,"* explained Victor. *"El vive muy lejos de aquí en el arroyo* (He lives far up in the arroyo)."

Juan seemed startled, like a wild thing. With spare frame and gaunt cheeks, he thrust out to me a copybook—and on page 1 were *A*'s; on page 2, *B*'s—the lesson of yesterday. Some of the letters were backward, some sideways, but all were carefully, painstakingly done.

"Quieresa ir a la escuela (Do you want to go to school)?" I had asked.

"Sí, por favor (Yes, please)," was his eager reply.

His sisters, Yolanda and María, had been my next enrollees, and after some regular sessions on the beach or the patio outside our bedroom, I thought I should visit the Geraldo home. The girls needed some fluoride to protect their teeth, and Juan needed more food. Chavalo had taken me by pickup truck some five miles back into the arroyo.

Juan's home was made of palm fronds. The floor was dirt. Chickens, the pig, and a small goat had free run of the area. Besides Juan and his sisters, there were three younger children and an infant.

So I said that we needed an assistant for Chavalo, and would Sra. Geraldo permit Juan to work for us if we provided lunch? Lunch quickly stretched to three meals and food for home, and now the joy was to watch this mind grow. He had intense concentration, a fierce desire, and sweetness too. The children loved to play with him.

Now Harry tossed him a small flat stone which he skipped expertly over the water. *"Seis. Es más que tú puedes, Harrito* (Six. That's more than you can do, Harry)," he challenged.

"Pues, mira Juan, mira (Look, Juan, look)! I'll skip this one ten times"—but not so. Harry's attempt flopped weakly; the stone foundered and sank.

Rosie just watched the boys, her deep blue eyes measuring, wondering. Then we began the slow trek up the hill, and Juan, while carrying towels with Harry, explained the differences in the cactus. The *carambullo* was like a candelabra, the *viznaga,* a big barrel with red flowers. The tiniest plant around the palms was *hielito*—little ice plant.

"Are you going to take him home?" she asked Bing.

"I'd love to, but Mexico needs men of his stamp. Tony Ruffo in La Paz, who owns the fishing fleet and the big general store, has promised us that he will see to Juan's higher education. I'd love to see how he turns out. Say, why don't you slip into something Andalusian. We'll go down and take on a little *comida mejicana* at the hotel."

"The main reason you want Juan and the others in higher education is because our classes are conducted in your bedroom."

"Yes, it gets a bit crowded in there and I object to my pipes being used to blow bubbles."

Twenty minutes later Rosie came from her room—a pastel vision in cool blue silk.

"My, you're all gussied up tonight."

"Oh, just a little thing I dug out of my musette bag."

"Well, here's a hibiscus to tuck behind your ear . . ."

"Or carry in my teeth?"

"It might hamper your dialogue."

"Just give me the hibiscus. I'll think of someplace."

"That's what I'm afraid of. Listen, Rosie, this is a family club, and besides, you're not wearing a bare midriff."

We piled into the beach buggy and bumped our way to the hotel for Consuelo's *cena* (dinner). *Qué sabrosa* (How delicious)! *Albóndiga* soup, broth with tiny meatballs, then a dish ("The size of home plate," moaned Bing) with *taco,* enchilada, frijoles, *arroz, chalupa,* and chicken *mole.*

The dining room was not crowded. Many guests were still

swimming in the pool; some were sipping Chacho's Margaritas with their feet propped up on the fountain rim.

In the game room domino, pitch, and chess games were in full swing, and at the bar Chiquito, the waiter, was listening politely to all kinds of wild fish stories. His enigmatic smile never revealed just how much English he understood or believed.

"*Qué tal?* How are you, Bing?" A handsome man in white slacks and shirt open to the fourth rib came from the kitchen. "I just had a bowl of soup. Man, I'm tired—flew to San Diego this morning; back here tonight. Now I have to take off for Palmilla."

At this moment he noticed Rosie, and saying, "Maybe I'll go to Palmilla tomorrow," he flopped into a chair.

Bing said, "Rosie, this is Rod Rodriguez."

Rod rose, clicked his heels, and kissed her hand.

"You mustn't be misled, even though he acts like the gayest kind of a *caballero*," continued Bing. "He owns the place—not only owns it, but designed and built it."

"Oh come on, Bing," demurred Rod.

"Not only this place, but Palmilla on the tip and Hacienda Cabo San Lucas at the Cape: three lovely hotels, done with taste and appropriate to the environment. And if you knew how hard it was—flying in materials, equipment, and supplies, teaching the *trabajadores* the work that needed to be done . . ."

"Now Bing—*nada, nada, nada.*"

"I really think you did these things to prove to your dad—General Rodriguez was President of Mexico, Rosie—that you too could serve your people."

Rod laughed an embarrassed laugh and said depreciatingly, "What else can an aged test pilot do?"

"Not only a test pilot, Rosie, but years in the Canadian and American Air Forces, instructing and flying, and, since the war ended, seven days a week in the air between here and San Diego, here and Mexico City, and countless other places. I really think he's logged more hours aloft than Bob Hope and Howard Hughes combined."

Rod dug the toe of his huarache in the sand, looked up, and said brightly, "*Amigo,* I may have you do my biography."

Bing asked, "Can I tell all?"

"*Nunca, nunca!*" Rod screamed. "I'd be flooded with law-suits."

"Braggart," said Bing.

"My, Mr. Rodriguez, you certainly have had a thrilling and colorful career. I'd love to hear about some of your exploits during the war—aerial dogfights, crash landings, and thrilling escapes from disaster."

"What's this girl doing, Bing," said Rod. "Putting me on?"

"No," said Rosie, with obvious sincerity, "I just know you must have had many harrowing adventures."

"I suppose," said Rod, after a moment's thought, "the time when I was in the biggest sweat was right down here in Baja California. I had just finished building the hotel, and a couple of cottages here at Las Cruces, and it seemed to me it would be a very nice idea to have some game native to the area around the hotel grounds to kinda establish some color. So one day I took off in my little Cessna 140 for Santiago.

"There was no strip at Santiago then, and it was necessary for me to make a landing on the main street, after dragging the place once and alerting the citizens. This was an unusual enough event to attract quite a crowd, and after making known my wants, I was able to collect a yearling deer and a cageful of blue quail.

"I tied the deer's feet around the copilot's seat and stuck the cage of quail in that little space that's behind the pilot's seat.

"After seemingly endless *gracias*'s and *adiós*'s, I took off again off the main street and circled the little pueblo. At about two thousand feet all hell broke loose. The deer had managed to free his hind legs, and kicked a big hole in the quail cage, and the quail were flying all over the tiny cabin while the deer was lashing about trying to free his front feet.

"I tell you, I was busy as a one-legged man at a pants-kicking contest, trying to hold that deer down with one hand before he kicked the panel to pieces, and stuffing the quail back in the cage whenever I could get a second's respite.

"Somehow or other I got the plane back down on the street again, unloaded my recalcitrant group of passengers, and told the *jefe* I'd send the truck for them in a few days.

"That, my dear Miss Clooney, was my most harrowing experience in the air. Sounds funny now, but at the time, it was *muy serio.*"

Bing said, "Now, if you ladies can still walk after all this food, I've a small surprise for you at the house."

Rod joined us on the ride home and we all walked to the front patio overlooking the ocean. The full moon lighted our way; the plumeria perfumed our path, and the soft strumming of guitars gave the surprise away.

"Oh, Bing, the *mariaches*. That's too much!"

"You don't think I'd let you come down here without a little something special, do you?"

Rod held out a chair for Rosie; then started to sit next to the beautiful visitor—but his gallant plans went awry when the children came running in slippers and robes.

"*Qué tal,* Rod? It's great to see you!" Then Mary Frances sat on his knee, Nathaniel in the chair beside him, and Harry curled up next to his "girl friend," Rosie.

Rod teased his *amigita* by testing her new-found Spanish. "*Digame,* Maria Francesca. What do you say in the morning?"

"*Buenos días,*" she responded.

"*Muy bien.* Now what do you say after noon?"

"*Buenas tardes.*"

"*Fantastico!* What do you say at night?"

There was a pause of uncertainty, then she lisped hopefully, "It's gettin' dark?"

Nathaniel curled up in my lap and then the entertainment began. "*Naranjas dulces, limón partidas, dame a un abrazo, qué yo te pido . . .*" they sang and the children were spellbound. "*Guadalajara,*" "*Borrachito Me Voy*" followed. The haunting Latin melodies wafted down the hill to Casa Fisher; a volleyball game on the beach ceased, and the *marineros* listened too. The stars seemed very near, and miraculously we could follow the path of a satellite tracking its way across the sky.

Rosemary and Bing, singers of a sort themselves, listened raptly to the trio from La Paz. Not a word was spoken, but a tapping foot or the click of a finger revealed they were with it.

With *Coo-curu-coo coo, Paloma,* sung very plaintively, very softly, the serenade ended. The children were sound asleep.

Bing whispered, "Do you like Segovia?" in his inimitable patois. Their eyes lit up, and soon Bing had pulled out some treasured albums. The men huddled around the phonograph savoring the master in Bach and de Falla. Then: "But you have to get back to La Paz. Here—take the discs. Hope you enjoy them as we've enjoyed you."

They whispered, *"Gracias. Adiós."* And they left by taxi. Rod carried Mary Frances, Bing took Harry, and we tucked them into bed. Rosie and I fixed the laundry basket for Nathaniel by my bed, and he just fit. Then back out on the patio.

"Do you think Nathaniel will be all right in the basket?" asked Bing.

"Darling, he'll be right beside me . . ." I started.

"Oh, that's a help! Once you're asleep, he could be carried off by the coyotes and you'd never turn over. If these children survive with such a negligent nurse for a mother, it'll be a miracle."

There was a gleam in Bing's eye, a mock seriousness in his voice portending gross slander. I'd have to hear all over again.

"Rosie, let me tell you what kind of nurse she is. You won't believe such dereliction of duty."

"What did she do, Dad? Give you a leaky hot-water bottle?"

"Don't be fresh! We were going to Santiago for a white-wing shoot a couple of weeks ago. We took off with Rod about five thirty in the morning. It's a farming area, a rich valley about thirty-five minutes flying time away. They grow *chicharos,* a delicious green pea there, and the birds are so thick, they become a serious menace to the crop."

"So you, the farmer's friend, have to help out?"

"Always available in a national emergency—though I love a barbecued dove as well as the next fellow. Now, we've made some good friends there, Sr. and Sra. Osuna. Sr. Osuna took us to the ranchos where we had a good shoot, and at about ten o'clock we went along to his home, where Sra. Osuna was waiting with guacamole and tortillas."

"I know. Kathryn forgot the Alka-Seltzer!"

"Far, far worse! See how she cringes now—guilt-laden, with beaded brow and palsied hand. Oh, I tell you this was a heinous offense."

"She should get the rack," said Rosie darkly.

"I was thinking of the knout." And he continued, "Rod doesn't shoot, but he collected us at the air strip at eleven. I was feeling a little puny, a little strange . . ."

"It was a hot flash," I muttered.

"No interruptions, Miss Nightingale! We drove up to the house and now I felt like a dog passing a peach seed. I asked for the thermometer—certainly a routine request to one who is studying to be a nurse. And—are you ready for this? She forgot to bring one from the States. While I stood quivering with the ague, and in amazed disbelief, she put her paw on my burning forehead and said, casually, 'You're pretty warm.'

"Then I asked for some aspirin, only to learn she had given it to a woman with a toothache down in the village. She offered me an antibiotic which as anyone with the most cursory knowledge of medicine will aver, has no effect on vital diseases, such as colds, flu, bubonic plague, galloping crud. . . ."

"Mumps, chicken pox . . ."

"Don't be a knowledge dropper!" he snapped. Rosie and Rod were enjoying this big scene from King Lear.

"But wait—this was serious. I went to bed, hoping that my beloved would stay near to observe, cool my brow with cold packs, ply me with soup and soothing medications, see that my rest was undisturbed. What does she do? She wanders off and goes to sleep in the guest room. I had to answer the door when the *marineros* came to deliver parts for the boat; two busloads of tourists came up from the hotel to see the house and get my autograph; I had to fix my own lunch, and," he finished petulantly, "there was a passing burro who clomped up on the patio and proceeded to devour the bougainvillaea under my window."

"Listen, Bing, do you think we should let her give all these vaccinations if she's so careless?" asked Rod.

"Oh, she'll stay awake for that. Any loose child is bound to get stuck with her around." And he gave me a short right to the shoulder, the closest he would come to a public show of affection.

"Well, *amigo,* if you think it's safe, we'll have the Tine T.B. tests at the hotel next weekend. Dr. von Borstel will be here too —*bueno.* Got to go. *Adiós todos.*" He kissed Rosie's hand again, and was gone.

Rosie looked at her hand as though he'd just put a cabochon ruby on her finger and said, "He'd be a riot in Maysville, Kentucky."

Next morning the saucy cardinal had wakened our special guest by pecking at her windowpane. The quail in the laurel tree were driven out by a firm shake because they were making such a racket with their courting shenanigans. With injured dignity, they marched to the leak in the water tank to drink—and we gathered for breakfast.

There was no time to observe the hummingbirds next; no time to marvel at the blanket of bougainvillaea which shaded our outdoor *comedor* (dining room). We were on our way for a day at Cerralvo Island.

The *María Francesca* took us for marlin first, and Rosie caught one in fifteen minutes, using ten-pound test. She released it to cheers from the gallery—Bing and I and two small spectators in life jackets tied to the transom step. Nathaniel had stayed at Casa Crosby.

Then she and Harry caught *cabrillo,* a bass, near the rocks. Pelicans told us by their dive-bombing where fish were to be found but they couldn't help bring in the 90-pound grouper Bing latched onto. That took an hour, some tired shoulder muscles, and some colorful language.

We searched for shells on the sand spit and found a pink murex with its operculum intact, and a batch of cone shells.

We lunched near an old shark fisherman's camp, just a palmetto windbreak against the night's chill, with the ashes of a campfire to leeward.

Then we headed for home, slowly. Porpoises frolicked around the boat. The water was green and serene and so inviting that when we reached the muey, we all took another swim.

This was glorious. We were exhausted, yet Rosie looked like a teen-ager. Bing was so right. This was exactly what she needed —some time away from family and tinseltown.

We climbed into the beach buggy and started up the hill for Casa Crosby. Ladies in the back, Harry and his dad up front.

We bumped along and Harry turned to tease Mary Frances. When he did so, he let go of the little handbar, and when he let go of that little handbar, my heart stopped. It was almost in slow motion.

Silently, so slowly, his body drifted through the air and went down. There was a bump as the car went over a large rock—or was it a rock? The insane thought flashed across my mind. This of course couldn't be. I always insisted that my children use safety belts when in any car, even in the back of the station wagon. This was not happening. There wasn't even a door on this car.

Then reality took over. Oh, God, not that! Not my baby! Please don't let him be hurt. Please don't let him be hurt. The silence was terrible. The car came to a halt, but no word was spoken by anybody.

Bing and I ran to the little body, covered with dirt, lying by the side of the road. Rosie grabbed Mary Frances by the arm and started walking up the road, away from what was to come.

We huddled over the little boy. Blood was everywhere. Had the car really struck him, or were these just scratches from hitting the rocks and pebbles by the side of the road?

He wasn't unconscious. That was good. He was bellowing like a young bull. Not only bellowing, but the things he was screaming, things that made it impossible for me to blame myself or Bing to blame himself for this terrible thing.

"I'm sorry, Mommy, I didn't hold on. I'm sorry. I'm sorry. I'll hold on next time."

We were stunned for a second. Then I said breathlessly, "Let's get right to the airport and get him to La Paz."

Bing answered firmly, "We have to get him cleaned up first. It looks bad around the eye."

I'd been afraid to look at the eye. I was afraid he'd lost it. I was afraid to clean off the blood for fear there would be more than just dirt underneath.

Bing carried him tenderly to the car and put him in my lap. We eased up to the house hating every bump and turn in the road. We kept him perfectly flat on the sink drain and washed his head. Then I saw his arm. We'd run over his arm. It was split right down to the bone.

Rosie helped hold him and I was suddenly three people. One of me was carefully, calmly cleaning sand, dirt, and rocks from around and in the eye. Another voice way inside was crying, "Oh, my poor, beautiful baby. My lovely baby with his big brown eyes. How will he look after this? How will he look?" And still a third voice was saying, "You ass. Shut up. He's not dead. He's got at least one eye. Maybe both. He's got a brain. He never passed out. He didn't even have a concussion. Now shut up and do what you have to do."

Bing was very close. Then he quickly collected the pilot and in three minutes the plane was ready. I had looked at Rosie for one anguished moment. She said, "You're doing fine, Katie. I'll handle things here. Mary Frances and Nathaniel and I will be all right. Now go on." But she couldn't look at Harry.

Five minutes later—La Paz. The taxi took us and our precious bundle to one hospital. No, the doctor wasn't there. Then to the next. A phone call home, and there was Dr. von Borstel, a German who spoke Spanish, English, French, and Italian fluently. A man of science, a kind man.

He took our baby and said, "We'll give him X rays first."

Nothing at all was broken. The doctor's soft voice was saying, "I'm sorry about this surgery room. Our new social security hospital is not quite finished, and this one is on its last legs."

The woman with the mop had just finished cleaning. I asked, "Where do we scrub for surgery, Doctor?"

"Right here in the sink."

We washed our hands as best as we could, and then I was

holding Harry's hand while Dr. von Borstel worked. The black sand had ground down right into the skull. It was ugly. Ugly and painful. Harry was in shock. Then the stitches with coarse black thread—"It's all we have. I'm sorry, Sra. Crosby."

Bing was standing by the fountain with the pilot—waiting, waiting. Dr. von Borstel said, "Would you like to stay with Harry tonight? There is a cot by the baby's bed and one single bed." Of course. Nothing could have made us leave him.

All night we were together in Harry's room—Bing, our first baby, and I.

Dr. Martinez, the young intern from Guadalajara, came in and sat with us for an hour. Dr. von Borstel checked after he'd had his dinner. Then we three were alone.

I lay in the bed right next to Harry, my hand touching him. Bing took walks for some fresh air. He said the stars were very bright. It was a clear night. We'd probably be able to fly in the morning, if the night went well.

Then the mosquitoes started to bite. I tried to brush them away. I tried, but they kept coming. Finally we all fell into a troubled sleep.

About one o'clock in the morning we heard a strange buzzing overhead. Not more mosquitoes! I couldn't stand it. But it was louder. Strange, nobody flies at night. It's a rule in Mexico.

Ten minutes later Rod Rodriguez came in. "All right, what happened? I've got to take the news back so Rosie and the rest of us can get some sleep. Everyone's waiting to know what happened."

"He'll be all right."

"*Gracias. Adiós.* See you in the morning." And he was gone.

At dawn, Dr. von Borstel affirmed that Harry could travel. "He'll be all right, *senora*. That is an ugly scar, but he has his eye."

We flew back over the mountain to Las Cruces. Rosie met us. "Harry, how's my beau? We were waiting for you all night. Now come sit on my lap." She held Harry all the way back to Casa Crosby while I cried silently into Bing's shoulder. One night's stoicism was about my limit.

"Bing, I've been on ship-to-shore radio this morning; you know Harry's doctor takes care of our boys too. Well, he'll be at the airport when you get there. I said you'd probably leave here at nine thirty and arrive in Santa Monica at two thirty. Was that right? And I'm all packed."

"But Rosie, you can't leave like this. You came here for a rest," protested Bing.

My cry had done me a world of good and my faculties were returning.

"Darling, if you can keep the ship-to-shore communications open and don't mind chasing after Mary Frances and Nathaniel, Rosie and I will handle Harry."

Harry opened his one unbandaged eye and tried to smile. "Aunt Rosie'll handle me, Mom. I'm her beau, you know!"

CHAPTER 9

How To Be Happy Though Married

We were in Hillsborough in the schoolroom at the top of the stairs. It was a Spartan room, furnished with three little desks and long, long stacks of books. It was a perfect length for our 16-mm projector, if either Bing or I could ever learn how to load the machine. Although it was described as automatic, it wasn't automatic enough for us.

The three children were working quietly. I sat down next to Nathaniel Patrick. "Look, Mommy, is the *M* right?"

"Perfect, Nathaniel. Down, down—slant in to the center, and then slant backwards to the center. That's the way. That's a beautiful *M*—I've never seen such a gorgeous *M,* and the way you colored the monkey! You want to try something new? Here we are—why don't you read this? Just the first page. What does L say?"

"*Uuuuu . . .*"

"That's right. Now this word is *look.* Can you write it on the blackboard?" He did, and it was recognizable. "Want to try the next page?"

"Oh—not *ho,* honey."

The other children had read this book to him since he was two. He'd always looked at the colored pictures and never bothered about the words, but now suddenly the words meant something. He was no more surprised than I was.

"That's Sally."

"Yes, I know—that's the picture of Sally. Now see if you can find her name."

"Right there."

"Right, Nathaniel. Want to try another page?"

As he groped for each word, I studied this cherub of ours. He was developing such tact.

Last Monday, when I was chief cook and bottle washer, breakfast had been a decidedly qualified success. The cereal was fine, the eggs were scrambled well, the bacon was crisp, but I had managed to burn the toast. Harry and Mary really lit into me for poor performance.

"Ah, Mom, you can't cook anything. Anyone can make toast."

"Mother, the toast is terrible."

Even Bing chimed in. "Honey, is there any zwieback out there? This is inedible."

I brought a fresh loaf of bread and the guilty toaster to the table and was just about ready to throw in the towel. At this low moment in my morning, Nathaniel looked at me solemnly and comforted, "You can't cook, Mommy, but you're nice."

The book went on and on. When Nathaniel reached page 30— "Look, Spot, Jane, Sally, Mother, Daddy"—I signaled to Mary Frances and Harry, who came over quietly, eagerly. Nathaniel began to sense that something unusual was taking place.

" 'Up, up, up,' she said. Then go da-da-da . . ."

"Which way is the opposite of 'up,' Nathaniel? It starts with a *duh—duh*."

"Down, down?"

"That's right." He reached the last page. "Oh, oh, oh!"

Wild cheers broke out from Harry and Mary Frances, and old Mom. I grabbed my pencil and wrote the date on the flyleaf of our book, and Nathaniel said, "May I write my name now, Mommy?"

"You certainly may, Nathaniel. You have read this book today, your very first."

We had to hold our celebration in abeyance while he methodically printed N-A-T-H-A-N-I-E-L. Then we played ring-around-a-rosy and squeezed him within an inch of his life. He was red in the face and squealed, "Sister hugs too hard." Then more ring-around-a-rosy, and they all landed in a heap on the floor.

Cindy, the little Labrador retriever, looked up from her corner by the big world globe, cocked her head, decided we were crazy, and pretended to go back to sleep.

"All right, darling, now it's time to go to bed. You've done a big day's work."

He started to the door, grinning as if he'd just written the Declaration of Independence. "You come right back here and clean your desk before I skin you alive." One quick look at my face and he grinned wider. "You wouldn't skin me alive now I can read, would you, Mommy?"

He put away the paper with the *M* for Monkey, and the phonetics book. I turned out his study light. He came over to me cozily, "Mommy," he said. I was checking some other work, and he took my face in his hands and turned it toward him, putting his nose about three inches from mine. "Mommy, can I take my book to show Daddy?"

"Yes, love. Now scat." I moved forward for a kiss and he backed off and shouted in horror, "No kissing," and ran for the door. I caught him in time for a quick hit on the bottom as he went out. Then I had a moment of panic, "Nathaniel, stop! Don't you dare run down those stairs, you hear me? You walk."

He walked the first six steps before I could hear his feet speeding up to a quicker pace. *Silence*—my heart stopped—then came the familiar crash at the bottom of the stairs, but not the alarming one I feared. It sounded as if he were on his feet. Another instant of waiting. No screams, and footsteps going off. Yes, he'd made it again.

Mary Frances was still continuing the celebration with Harry, giggling and rolling around on the floor with Cindy now. "All right, now, back to work," I said. There was quiet for ten whole minutes. Mary Frances was trying to figure out maps and roads in her *Weekly Reader*. She had a big hole in the toe of her shoe.

"Okay, sweetheart, sit up straight. You'll never get any blood to your head if you scrunch down like that."

"Which way is east, Mommy?"

"East is your right hand, west is your left. Now which is your right hand? No, no, not that one. The *right* one. Oh, dear, sweetheart, when you try, you can give a good imitation of a not-very-bright little girl."

She looked totally crestfallen, so I gave her a little hug. "There are times, of course, when you're absolutely adorable. Now see if you can finish this quietly."

I went back to my chair to organize work for the class I was teaching next day. Cindy put her nose on my foot. A chance to think for a second anyway. Oh, Mary Frances was going to be such a challenge, such a wonderfully exciting challenge. She wasn't quite so cuddly as the two boys. She was always lovable, but when she climbed up on my lap, inevitably she would step on my toe and stick her elbow in my ribs.

Both Bing and I had felt so concerned when he had decided to do a film about fishing in England. He took me along. Mary Frances' birthday was the fourteenth of September, and we wouldn't be back for it. When the day came around, we were way up in a tiny and delightful village in the north of England called Greystoke. We decided we should try and get a call through to her. No simple thing, this. When, after considerable delay, we finally got through to Hillsborough, we learned she had gone to school. Of course, when we got through to the school, she was in class, so we asked if she could be brought to the office of the principal, our friend Mr. Brown. Finally we heard her piping voice over all those thousands of miles, "Hello, Daddy." When Bing had swallowed the catch in his throat, he sang the traditional "Happy Birthday" song to her. There was a moment's silence, and then Mary Frances said, "Oh, that's lovely, Daddy. Now sing it again for Mr. Brown!" Even at those prices, there had to be an encore.

At the far end of the attic, there was a silence, which meant that Harry was daydreaming again. I walked down and sure enough, Harry was staring out the window with a faraway expression in his eyes.

"Have you finished your report on whales, honey?"

"Here it is, Mom."

I read the paper, or rather, I decoded it. It was a maze of ups and downs, detours and erasures, but the thoughts were splendid once you got them properly assorted and assembled. "Harry, I think this is a fine paper. You've conceived it beautifully, but it's illegible."

"Ah, Mom, you mean I have to write it over again?"

"Yes, you have to write it over again until it's more presentable. And if once more will do it, fine. But if it takes twelve more times, I'll wait here for that."

The storm clouds started to gather. He wrecks me when his face clouds up like that. "Don't you sull up on me, young man. Any boy who will pick a fight with a fourth-grader is much too old to cry when he has to copy a paper over. Now get with it, and if you finish on time, we can do some pages of cursive writing. And, Harry, you must start by sitting up straight." He assumed the proper posture reluctantly and started again. Oh, if only I didn't have to nag him so much. I knew my voice was sharp and edgy; I was tired. The day had started at six thirty. Somehow there hadn't been any time at all to slow down.

After what seemed an eternity, the report was finished. "Well done, darling. That's very nice. Oh, Harry, for heaven's sakes, don't wrinkle it up."

"Mom, you know I'm going shooting with Dad this weekend? He's already promised me. But, you know, I don't think it's fair. Last time we went out I shot at lots of pheasants, and I think I hit some, but you know Dad's got about fifty BBs in each shell that he shoots and I only have one BB in my gun. I think I should shoot fifty times for every time he shoots."

"Did you tell that to your father?"

"Yes, and you know what he did?"

"What did he do?"

"He gave me a big hug and he laughed, right in front of Trader Vic. A father shouldn't hug a fella in public, should he?"

"You bet he should, Harry."

"Can I go down and talk to Daddy about hunting?"

"You may, if he's not watching the ball game, but be up-stairs for bed in ten minutes."

"Mom, how old do we have to be before we can watch TV on school nights?"

"One hundred and ten." I smacked his jeans. "Now, get out of here." Then, as an afterthought, "Whoops, come back and clean up your desk and turn out the light." A quick flurry and he was gone, for those special ten minutes with his father.

Two lights out and the big attic looked kind of spooky. But Mary Frances was still working away. "Come on, darling, I think it's time you went to bed."

"Oh, but Mom, I'm not quite finished. Just this page."

"All right."

"Mother." Here it comes, something very formal and grand. "Mother," she repeated, "are you going to give your anatomy lecture again in school?"

"Well, honey, I haven't been asked."

"But I was sick last year when you lectured to the second grade on the urinary tract, and I didn't hear it."

"Well, Mary Frances, all I did was take Gray's *Anatomy* to school and then on the blackboard I drew the kidneys, like lima beans, and the ureters, which look like little straws or tubes, and the bladder, which is a kind of balloon in the middle, and then we discussed the differences between boys and girls, and you know them. Besides, you can have Gray's *Anatomy* any time you want it, although you'd better let me take it off the shelf next time. If it ever falls on your foot, it'll break four metatarsals."

She finished the page, turned out the light, put her books in the desk tidily, and marched out of the room regally, calling Cindy to follow her.

Downstairs we went through their rooms. Mary Frances has pretty flower-printed draperies which she chose herself, two "gorgeous" canopy beds that she swings on only occasionally, and Nana's doghouse from our production of *Peter Pan*. The boys' room adjacent has Captain Hook's ship, lifted from the same play, on either end of the sofa, and in that ship, the hold of which is now a toy box, creepy crawlers lurk among the balls, bats, mitts, and dinky cars. Over Harry's bed hangs a forty-three-pound marlin caught when he was five; over Nathaniel's, a fierce-looking rooster fish caught with a little assistance from Dad.

"Your teeth, Mary Frances, up and down, don't forget." Then I leaned over the banister, calling, "Boooyyys," in a muted scream. They burst in with a great charge, Remus following, and for a moment I yearned for a lion tamer's whip, what with dogs and boys and banging doors and drawers, and faucets left running and toothpaste caps lost down the toilet.

Suddenly, as if a wand had waved, peace descended, and three candidates for the Littlest Angel Award knelt by the bed. Prayers were extrapious, including a seasonal "and keep Santa safe," and then all three slipped silently into their beds.

Harry began to read *Comeback,* the story of his grownup friend, Ken Venturi; Mary Frances became immersed in *Little Women;* and Nathaniel chose *Happy Birthday to You* because it was nearly the birthday of the Baby Jesus. I read to him in a somnolent monotone, but though Nathaniel's eyelashes fluttered, he hung on until the very end. He was warm and cuddly while I read, and I savored this, knowing that in the morning he would be Daddy's big boy again, fiercely independent, stubborn, scornful of a mother's embrace.

I tucked him in, yearning for one more hug but afraid to push my luck. Then over to Harry.

"Only five more pages in this chapter, Mom."

"All right, son. Turn out your light then, will you?"

A perfunctory kiss, but then a warm hug from this tall, lean young man. His eyelashes were so long and curly, and his ears were just like his dad's.

Then across the way to Mary Frances, who had both Remus and Cindy at the side of her bed, petting one with each hand while reading. She must have turned pages with her tongue.

"Dearest, it's about that time."

"Yes, Mother." And she turned down a huge dog-ear, ignoring the two book markers on her bedside stand. I needed only to raise an eyebrow and she quickly put things right.

A warm hug, a sweet kiss, and "Good night."

Cindy, Remus, and I walked on downstairs. I mustn't go too soft over that little dog. I was the one who always felt dogs should stay in the yard where they belonged, and had been so jealous of Remus when he first took over our family. I'd never forget when up at the ranch, I'd walked in to find the big black Labrador reclining peacefully on a gorgeous new patchwork quilt on our bed, his filthy hind feet athwart the turquoise pillows.

I screamed at him, but Bing said, "Ah, but doesn't he look comfortable up there? He's tired; we've had a hard day in the field."

"Well, he can be tired in the gun room, where dogs belong."

"Don't be a shrew," Bing came back. "This dog has broken ice to retrieve ducks all over the lake. He's been fighting his way through miles of muddy tules picking up 'sailers.' "

"And he's packed most of the mud in our bedroom and spread it all over my beautiful quilt."

"Well, he's a good dog, and I love him."

"I would, too, if he'd ever bring a duck to me. Why does he have to take all of the game to you?"

"Because he's *my* dog; that's what it means when you have a dog."

Now I had my dog, Cindy. She was a daughter of Remus and was only the nicest dog that ever lived.

She had produced puppies, six lovely, healthy pups, and since it was cold and rainy when they were born, we brought them in almost immediately from the kennels to my office. All was well until they got big enough to climb out of the basket. Then I realized with horror that they were too young to be vaccinated for distemper, and that if we kept them outside, where it was still cold, undoubtedly they'd get it. I was stuck with them for six weeks.

Bing bore up grimly, but for the last few days he kept walking by my office, opening and closing the door abruptly, flaring his nostrils, and muttering, "Smells like an abattoir. Get them out, out!"

"Would you turn these poor helpless infants out in the cold?"

He threw up his hands and stalked off to the library with Remus at his heels. Cindy and I had a few more chores to finish.

Gingerly I slid open the door to my office, a treasure of a room to me. It had originally been a gentlemen's smoking room, and the wood paneling and tiny fireplace were compatible with Barnaby Conrad's portrait of Bing in shooting clothes over the mantel. My small Georgian desk was overflowing with clutter, the small sofa heaped with copies of unread *Nursing Journal,* unread newspapers from Texas, unanswered mail. And over all this my portrait as Raina in the Shaw play looked down prissily in the flowered hat, leaning with elegant poise on a fragile parasol.

Had that been I only two summers ago? I opened the paneling to the hidden fridge for a can of pineapple juice and stared at a caricature of "The Divine Sarah" on the other wall. That was much closer to me now. The eyes were black holes under a mass of spiderwebby black hair. The thin mouth revealed the exhaustion I felt.

"Stop biting my ankle! You little rascals!" I forgot about the juice and started to round up escapees from the canine prison we'd made out of the right half of the room. Cindy's sextet tugged at my skirts, tugged at one another, emitting yips and squeals, then fell back into their bed a limp, exhausted mass of squirming black puppies.

I sat on the old music chair in front of my desk, picked up a pencil, and started to ponder. The Christmas party was the next thing. Without Mother here, I couldn't do all the cooking. I couldn't get her cornbread stuffing right, nor her banana cake with divinity icing. Last year had been simple. *Peter Pan* and the opening-night party was for my co-workers and their friends. But the pheasant I did for forty-five friends two years ago had given me the most pride. Mom and I put that party together, then Bing took us all out to carol. When we came back, there wasn't a bite of food left. I made scrambled eggs for Bing, who then sang English carols for the Fishers and their friends, Irish songs for Bridget and her friends. Jigs were danced, and Harry sang "Oh, Come, Little Children." That had been a gay, memorable time.

Now, this Christmas formal . . . Bing had suggested that Trader Vic should cater it. That made me feel guilty. But at least there would be no dishes to wash, and his squab *might* be as good as my pheasant. I'd have to finish up the menu and call the Trader tomorrow.

There would be two guests for each of our staff. Oh, dear, I hadn't really thought about their gifts enough. And I had promised to write a poem to make the gifts special. Well, better begin.

The first was a vase for our invaluable Norma:

> This little *Quelque Chose* is for
> Ten Thousand hours on the floor
> With brush and wax and polish pad
> Until the floors all gleam like mad.
>
> The bud vase with its sweet perfume
> Of roses newly come in bloom
> For saving pups from darkest doom
> As they leave droppings in my room.

Nobody would ever give me a Pulitzer Prize for it, but it would serve.

Next, for Alan Fisher, our butler—a more difficult one, because he does practically everything for us.

> Thank you for . . . now, where is that?
> Your brilliant talent . . . hunting hat? . . .
> I cannot stress—No! Not again!
> They must wear raincoats in the rain!
>
> The gratitude we feel enough.
> Change markets now—This steak is tough!
> We want to praise you to the sky—
> Good Lord, these bills are twice as high!
>
> I quote from Byron, Shelly, Keating . . .
> Now the boiler's overheating!
>
> In praise of you—unless I'm way off
> You never even take a day off.

Oh, well. And an ode to Bridget:

> In Erin's Isle there's none so fair
> No lass with shamrock in her hair
> No lady grand can ere compare with Bridget.
>
> Some clever girls can sew, they say,
> Some make a bed the four-square way,
> But none can do both every day, like Bridget.

Then for Deirdre, who has the hardest job of all:

> The lady in our nursery
>   has charge of three small storms.
>
> The squalls of early morning
>   she weathers in a breeze
> At hurricanes and tempests
>   she doesn't even sneeze

Another for Monica, and then to the hardest of all—a verse to go with Bing's gift. In New York I had found a pair of jade Buddhas that had once belonged to a king of Siam, carved, curiously enough, not in the Orient but in Russia. After a few false starts, I eked out some doggerel. Quite unworthy of these Fabergé treasures:

> The King of Siam
> Was an elegant man
> Though my knowledge of history is dim.
>
> Yet I'm happy to state
> On this Christmasy date,
> Darling, you're worth at least two of him.

Why such a collapse whenever Bing enters my so-called mind? What power does he have that dissolves all reason, all sense of syntax? I could forgive him the former, but not the latter. And what was I doing there, scribbling, while he was just fifteen steps down the hall?

I tried to close the door quietly, without rousing the puppies, but Cindy gave me an anguished look, realizing she would have to spend yet another sleepless night in their very close company.

"The joys of motherhood, my dear," I reminded her. She wagged a resigned tail, I thought, and settled down for the night.

I hurried toward Bing, then stopped. I felt that I had forgotten something, something vital. Oh well, as he said, I was overprogrammed as usual. It was a good day when I forgot only one thing.

I entered the library—a dark-paneled room with high ceilings and a big black marble fireplace. The fire was roaring cheerfully, and Bing was as usual transfixed by football on television, sunk deep in the yellow down-filled sofa, his feet propped up on the marble table.

"Good evening, darling."

"Ummmmmm," he replied.

I pulled a big cardboard box from a corner, and started applying pictures and sequins to styrofoam bases to make Christmas-tree ornaments.

"Darling?"

"Ummmmm."

"I'm teaching school tomorrow."

"Ummmmm."

"And darling, wouldn't it be lovely if I did a play in Chicago next summer, *The Guardsman*—the Lynn Fontanne part?"

"Ummmmm."

It was a game I played. There is nothing so intense as the concentration of a man on a sports event, whether televised, heard by radio, participated in, or viewed in person. Just any sport—it could be lacrosse, or dart throwing.

I could concentrate, too, when he wasn't near. But now, just being near him, I forgot whatever vital issues had been giving him concern.

The sofa he lounged on had been in the Los Angeles house. About a week before Harry was born, I had spent a sleepless night on it. I hadn't wanted to bother Bing because he had a full schedule the next day: recording in the morning, discussion about a new movie at noon, later a golf game with Bob Hope. I tiptoed downstairs and finally fell asleep on the living-room sofa. I woke up at noon and found him in the room, waiting. "Sleep well?" he had asked in an offhand manner. Only the spilled pipe tobacco and a stack of *Saturday Reviews* betrayed his vigil.

When his last kidney stone had been removed, I stayed in his room all night, and once he cried out for me. Later he denied the whole thing. "I was drugged," he said, shrugging.

Thinking of this, I passed behind him on my way to get more sequins for the ornaments, and bent to give him a kiss.

"Are you all right?" He emerged from his TV trance briefly, giving me a glance tinged with suspicion. I subsided into reverie.

Let him be Irish now! I had been there in the Sea of Cortés one sun-drenched day last year when he'd stated flatly, "You're mine—all mine." His blue eyes were more than rather romantic, and I suspect we'd have taken off for Tahiti then and there if a terrific wind hadn't come up, leaving the boat in nautical distress and me with a giant case of *mal de mer*.

Here in San Francisco the atmosphere was less romantic. Yet, when he was struggling into white tie and tails one night, mildly complaining, "I'll look like an unemployed magician in that top hat," he did pause at the door to say, "The things I do for you!" And he crooked his arm for my hand.

The fire had burned down to glowing warmth; the full moon shone through the cypress boughs. There was a hum, a click, and the TV was off. I wondered fleetingly who had won—more to the point, who had played? Back to the corner with the tree decorations.

"Come on, Remus, let's have a walk," said Bing.

Bing threw on a tweed jacket, I a loden coat, and with Remus we walked into the night. Eucalyptus trees filtered shafts of moonlight in our path. The air was cold and crisp and lovely. I hurried to keep up with my spouse and his black friend. He was striding out like an Olympic competitor in the heel-and-toe race. The quail in the oak tree fluttered to higher branches. Small clouds went scudding across the moon, and I could see our frosty breaths in the moonlight.

I shivered. South Texas blood is too thin for night marches in northern California, and I was relieved when we started back up the winding drive. Once Remus was inside, he went to his corner and plopped down exhausted. But I still had to hang up the coats (Bing had once called me slovenly), check the lights, and climb the stairs to our room.

The tiny reading lamps were alight on our headboard. The stack of books on Bing's table was tall, constantly changing; mine stayed constantly there and mostly unread.

Sconces of amber and crystal pears and purple grapes illuminated family pictures on the window ledge. Two old glass vitrines glowed with the sparkle of my Fabergé flowers, earned when I got my R.N. On a shelf by itself was Bing's medal. I went closer to read it again:

> "Presented to Bing Crosby in sincere appreciation of the outstanding performance on October 8, 1939. Attendance 187,730. The largest of all exhibition days at the Golden Gate International Exhibition."

I peeked through the drawn draperies. A wind was coming up, and it would be stormy by morning. Well, a high-necked nightie for me. High-necked, long-sleeved, and blue—with thick tennis sox to complete the ensemble. I scrubbed my face, then brushed out the dignified chignon. *Ow*—that rubber band hurt. I had to pass the mirrored door of the dressing room and I recoiled. I looked as if I were going to climb Everest. One of these days I must think of some more glamorous *costume de nuit*. But not tonight. Tonight I was too tired and cold to care.

Bing was waiting for me. We knelt a moment by the side of the bed for prayers. Then into bed. I lay there thinking: What was it that was nagging me? What had I forgotten?

Bing read *The Secret of Santa Vitoria* while I browsed through *Great Gardens of the World,* though it threatened to cave in my sternum. Would I ever pass even the simplest test as a gardener? My record there was a cipher, or worse—one very healthy, strange bluish plant had flourished from my planting. Bing said it was deadly nightshade.

I flipped the pages, hoping wanly I could fight off insistent lassitude until Bing turned out his reading light, our good-night signal.

Finally he put down his book. I eased mine onto the floor with a muffled thud, then turned to him. He was looking at me, his eyes inscrutable. "Kathryn, do you know what today is? Now don't strain yourself or cudgel your brain. Let me assist you with a few clues. First, you didn't have to drive the children up to the attic tonight—they have two weeks to do their work. Second, you're not teaching school tomorrow because school is closed for the holidays. Third, that party you've been planning for Christmas Eve is tomorrow—the twenty-fourth!"

"Oh, no," I gasped, "and I haven't called Trader Vic or the rental place!" Then it dawned on me. That's what had been worrying me. I hadn't planned the menu, or ordered the extra chairs.

I looked frantically at my nursing watch. It said 4:30, though it couldn't possibly be more than 10:30. Anyway, the chair place would be closed and Vic wouldn't have time to get a party ready. Maybe there were enough ducks in the deep freeze? I could do a duck *pot-au-feu,* and we could eat it picnic style. I started to lurch out of bed.

"Now don't panic. Vic and I arranged the menu a week ago, and Fisher has taken care of the extra furniture. I just thought you might like to know what day it was."

I subsided into the pillow, crushed. He gave me a light kiss, turned out the light. "Good night, dear."

I lay there chagrined, listening to the regular breathing by my side. If I couldn't even keep track of the day, how would I ever keep three children on the right track for twenty years or so? What would happen to them, poor things? How could I, hopelessly disorganized, even pretend to guide them, not to speak of the tremendously capable people in our household? Now they'd even had to arrange for their own Christmas party. And what an idea—I could never have made the *pot-au-feu*. The last time I'd tried cooking I had produced a very fancy dessert of glazed grapes, and the guests had looked as if they had all been smitten with lockjaw. The sugar was like mucilage, and they'd had to swallow the seeds.

I could never be the kind of wife Bing needed, wanted, deserved. All over the world they loved him, and he had to get stuck with a girl who didn't even know what day it was.

I felt cold—cold and insecure. My hand reached out and found his, waiting. "Come here, bloodless. You're as cold as a witch's. . . ."

"Darling!" I executed a combination slide-twist that had required years of diligent practice to master, and then was in my rightful place, head on his right shoulder, his arm circling my waist. Soon I was warm, very warm. I felt all the security any woman could ever need. Using my toes, I scuffed off the now unnecessary tennis socks. I lay there basking in utter contentment until Bing said softly, "Honey, are you awake? I wish we'd been married two years sooner."

Could it be? In spite of my inadequacies, in spite of everything, yes, now it was coming: The wild protestation of devotion for which I'd been waiting for nearly ten years. Now he'd tell me that though I was a good wife and mother, I was also the most provocative woman since DuBarry. Now he'd admit that I'd driven him to fits of insane jealousy, hidden only by his immense willpower. Now he would urge me to abandon instantly home, children, and career to run away with him to Pago Pago.

"Yes, my love. Why?" I purred.

"Harry would be two years older, and this spring I could take him hunting with me with a real gun, like a .22."